hummingbird

hummingbird

by Jude Angelini

A Rare Bird Book | *Los Angeles, Calif.*

THIS IS A GENUINE RARE BIRD BOOK

A Rare Bird Book | Rare Bird Books
453 South Spring Street, Suite 302
Los Angeles, CA 90013
rarebirdbooks.com

FIRST TRADE PAPERBACK ORIGINAL EDITION

Set in Minion
Printed in the United States

Cover art by Sage Vaughn
Illustrations by Ruby Roth

10 9 8 7 6 5 4 3 2 1

Publisher's Cataloging-in-Publication data
Names: Angelini, Jude, author.
Title: Hummingbird / by Jude Angelini.
Description: First Trade Paperback Original Edition | A Genuine Rare
Bird Book | New York, NY; Los Angeles, CA: Rare Bird Books, 2017
Identifiers: ISBN 9781945572593
Subjects: LCSH Angelini, Jude. | Comedians—United States—
Biography. | Disc jockeys—Biography. | American wit and humor.
| BISAC BIOGRAPHY & AUTOBIOGRAPHY / Entertainment &
Performing Arts
Classification: LCC PN1992.4.A2 A75 2017 | DDC 791.45/028/0922—dc23

For Thelma and Ev.
For Roger and Laura.
For the drive, for the thought, for the music, for the soul.

Contents

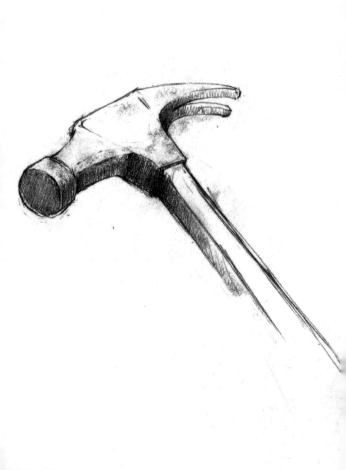

house calls

I'M 'BOUT TO TAKE mushrooms 'cause the ketamine's making me dumb. I thought for my new buzz I could just lay in bed, listen to music, and get gone. But when you do psychedelics you gotta make sure your shit's tight—your room's clean, your bills are paid.

I thought I was good. I wasn't.

I'm in bed tripping, thinking about life.

I'm pushin' forty, living with my sister. It's been four years since Julie's been gone. I'm still single. I'm snorting a gram of K a day, popping pills, running through chicks, and the girl I see the most is a twenty-three-year-old hooker. Fifteen hundred a trick but she fucks me for free.

I'm thinking to myself, *You might wanna girl and a healthier life, but you are what you do.* And I'm the fat guy shoveling cake in my mouth crying that I wanna be skinny.

When I sober up, I flush the rest of my Vikes down the toilet and dump the K. I call up all my girls and end it. I'm changing; a new leaf. I even go get my own apartment.

That lasts a year.

I'm at the dining table with a hammer beating a bag of ketamine. I lost all my drug connects, now I'm stuck with some bullshit from Pakistan. It ain't even flaky. It's granulated, like salt. Hard to blow, thus the hammer.

I pulverize it into a powder and snort it up. It's bullshit. No visuals, just dizzy. It's like I'm sniffing brain damage. I should probably do some more.

The call girl texts me. I haven't seen her in months. She's coming over. I straighten up the place, put on some jazz.

She shows up, her Benz dented and dirty. She's about thirty pounds bigger than last time, hands shaking, sweating. We go inside. I pour her a drink; we're sitting at the table.

I'm concerned. "What's up, girl? You okay?"

She says, "I'm fine, it's just hot in here."

I got all the windows open with the box fan blowing. I don't say nothing. She's looking into her drink, fanning herself with her hand.

I ask, "You been doing dope or anything?"

She says, "Nah. Not for a long time, but they still have me on methadone."

She started doing heroin when we stopped fucking—with her homegirl, full-blown with needles.

She was on it for a few months, went to kick and they put her on methadone.

I go to my room, I tell her to follow. I lie in my bed. She starts taking her clothes off.

I say, "Leave 'em on and lie down, we're not fucking."

She says, "It's 'cause I got fat, huh?"

I tell her, "That ain't it, you still got ass. I'm just worried about you. You look sick."

We're in bed. She's clammy and trembling, crying in my arms. They got her on 100 mg of methadone a day. It's been a year and they won't wean her off. She can't go nowhere. She's tethered to the clinic. Every day she's gotta come in for her dose or else she gets sick.

She ain't got no one to look out for her and the doc knows it, so she's gutting her, hiding behind that degree.

Her phone's stopped ringing. She's going broke. Nobody wants to fuck a fat call girl.

I say to her, "Look man, you gotta pay rent and you ain't got no other skills right now but fucking. You can't afford to be on this shit no more. And you prolly was doing dope 'cause you're miserable and shit, but you gotta get off this fucking methadone now. It's killing you. Figure out why you're sad later."

We come up with a plan: she's kicking it tomorrow, by herself. I give her some Phenibut and kratom for the withdrawals. She'll be alone in her apartment for the next month. She could use my help but this is as far as I go.

She's on her own. We all are.

She leaves.

That was heavy.

I'm rooting for her but I don't know if she'll make it.

I'll text her tomorrow.

I got shit to do tomorrow. I'm selling a leather midcentury armchair. I thought it was Danish 'cause I bought it off an old dude with a Nazi accent. It's not. It's just old. Nathan's coming over with his truck at eight in the morning to help me move it.

I should go to bed, but I can't get that booty call out my mind. That shit shook me, seeing her like that. All I wanted was some ass and I ended up with an intervention. I tell myself I deserve some more drugs because of what I just went through.

I open up the drawer next to my bed, pull out a plate with the Pakistani K on it, chop two monster lines, and snort 'em through my left nostril 'cause my right one's blown out.

I'm such a good friend.

It's coming on, the tingle and the vacant feeling. What the hell, let's do a couple more.

I do a couple more lines. I put on Supertramp— *Crime of the Century*. I'm at the end of the "School" song when I'm like, *I may have done too much.*

This happens a lot. I do too much a lot. My head goes underwater. I leave myself. Every time, I don't know if I'm gonna come back.

It feels like when I ODed on PCP. That wrecked me for months. I'm still not the same. I can't remember numbers, names are harder now, I can't organize my thoughts.

In the drawer next to my bed under the plate of ketamine are instructions of what to do with my writings if I cook myself. I wrote it while I was on K a couple years ago. Andrea's in charge.

Next to the instructions, there's a list of traits that I'm looking for in a woman. I wrote it after the breakup. It's my girlfriend wish list. It's coffee-stained and soaked in lube.

The song ends. And for a moment in the quiet of my room, I'm floating—blank, in the silence of my head. It's lonely there. The next song begins and I don't feel that anymore.

Alex texts me, "Yo."

He's going through a midlife crisis. He's pushing forty and fucking this twenty-one-year-old chola named Bunny.

I was at his place earlier. They were having a nice, quiet night in. Bunny baked homemade pizza. I'm over there talking up 2C-E and how awesome it is to fuck on. I run home. I front him four pills. He took 'em tonight.

He prolly wants to thank me. I text him back, "What's up?"

He hits, "Have you done this batch of shit? We're fucked up and not in a good way."

"Really? What's going on?"

He texts, "Yeah, it's pretty bad."

I get outta bed. "Hold up, I got something for you."

I throw on a T-shirt and some basketball shorts. I grab some Xanax off my dresser and the bottle of G. I find my keys and wallet. I call a car. He's there in three minutes. I do one more bump of K and leave.

I'm staggering down the hallway making a racket. I get to the car and stumble in; wallet, keys, and GHB come out of my pockets.

The driver's Armenian. The drive over's all EDM and cologne. I'm there in five minutes. He's revving the engine while I collect my shit from off his seat.

I get it. He peels off.

I'm inside. Bunny's curled up on the couch, rocking back and forth. She's in a T-shirt with her pussy out, but I'm a gentleman and don't notice. Alex is in a chair facing the door, shirt off, tatted up with a sumo ponytail. Wild-eyed, we look at each other and start laughing.

He says, "We're fucked."

I tell him, "You look awesome."

I take in the situation. Alex is freaking out and Bunny is freaking out too, which is making Alex freak out even more so that gets Bunny extra freaked.

I look around. It's like everything you could do to have a bad trip, they're doing. The place is a mess. The lighting's harsh. He's got no music on, just the drone of an industrial fan and an air conditioner. And it looks like they got *Me, Myself & Irene* on the TV with the sound down.

I start lighting candles and I turn off the floor lamp. I turn off the TV. I put on some Massive Attack to chill them the fuck out.

Bunny's hungry. I get her food. Bunny's cold. I get her a blanket.

She's in the Eames chair now. She says, "You like some weird shit. I'm just a little girl from the barrio. I'm not used to all this."

Alex is laying on the floor right where I was when I ODed on PCP. He says, "For real, I've done mushrooms, ten hits of acid, coke...ain't nothing like this, my nigga. This some white devil shit."

I say, "Nah, man, this just one of them science drugs. Just eat you some Xanax and chill."

Bunny piles on, "This shit is crazy. I don't know about you white motherfuckers. I'm used to doing regular drugs, like weed and meth."

I ignore it. "Have some water, you'll be okay."

I sit with them for an hour playing caregiver and DJ. They're both laid out, damn near naked, and I'm feeling like the third wheel. Maybe they should fuck. Fucking makes me feel better. I should go.

I tell 'em, "I'ma get."

Bunny protests. I insist. "Y'all should prolly just smash."

Alex tells Bunny to hit up his coke dealer. I'm trying to talk him out of it; I don't want his heart to stop. But he ain't listening to me, and I'm the one who got him here in the first place.

Alex says, "I got work in the morning. Will I be cool by then?"

"What time you work?" I ask.

"Around nine."

I look at my phone: it's four thirty-five.

He's stretched out, panting, trembling. He's bloated, looking like a dead animal on the side of the road. I've never seen nobody this fucked-up off of 2C-E.

I lie to him, "You'll be alright…"

He says, "I hope so."

I say, "And, uh, don't worry about paying for the pills. They're on me."

quasimodo

I'M AT THIS BAR called Satellite. It used to be Spaceland. It used to be cool. Used to be you could smoke there.

Now every time I'm here I end up seeing some late-thirties, never-gonna-make-it musician on stage, wearing a mall-kiosk fedora playing some shitty number.

I see my friend I'm s'posed to meet. It's her get-together. She's in town for the night. She's got five people around her, playing on their phones. Nobody's talking. I go speak. She says hi, tells me her friend's s'posed to play next.

Great.

I get the feeling this is less about her catching up with friends and more about getting people to a show.

It's bullshit. It gives these bad-singing mother-fuckers false hope. Some dreams are meant to be crushed. If they saw nobody liked them, they might stop wasting their money on studio time.

Now she's talking to a gay couple. I try and make conversation with the sassy one in lavender. But I don't think he understands me. He smiles politely then gives me his back.

I've been boxed out. I pivot. I pull out my phone and start drinking G.

I'm fucking around with this dating app. You look at pictures of chicks and like 'em or pass. And if both of y'all like each other you can holler.

At first, I was real earnest with my approach. I read their "About Me" section, weighed out the pros and cons, tried to project how it was gonna work out in six months, then made my choice.

It took an hour to like five girls. I'd go to bed feeling hopeful then wake up the next day and none of the chicks liked me back. And I'd head to work feeling rejected.

Now I just like 'em all and only holler at the cute ones. I got about forty chicks in my queue. But I've been slowing down lately 'cause I keep fucking these girls off here with herpes and not knowing it.

I've gotten away unscathed but there've been a lot of close calls. And I'm too old to be having that "I got something to tell you…" conversation with every new woman I'm 'bout to fuck.

Fifteen minutes into the set and the guy onstage finally starts singing a song I like.

I lean over to the purple gay dude. "Alright, this one jams."

He nods. "Yeah, it's an Oasis cover."

My phone buzzes. It's an alert from the dating app. This corny-looking white girl posing next to a dolphin hits me. We matched a week ago, but I haven't hollered yet 'cause I usually don't fuck with chicks posing with animals or on top of hills.

This is our first message.

I open it. It says, "Come over."

Late-night booty call from a young republican? I look up from the phone and mull it over. Jazz Hat's hittin' a guitar solo.

I write back, "Okay."

She shoots me her address.

I make a plan—I'ma run over there, eat that shit, beat the pussy up for like a half hour, get a cab back, catch the end of the show, pretend like I saw the whole thing, and tell 'em his last song was my favorite.

I leave the club. I got a nice little body buzz going but the G's got my head swimming. I'm dizzy. I may be too fucked up to bang. I sure would hate to hit some stranger's house with a limp dick, looking up from her crotch, mouth full of pussy and apologies, blaming the drugs.

I hit the 7-Eleven next door and pick up this fake-ass Viagra called Stallion or some shit. The dose is one pill. I pop two, then call a car and I'm on my way.

He drops me off in front of some fifties apartment building in Silver Lake. I dial her number. She buzzes me in. The hall's dreary. The carpet's stained. I walk

up a flight of steps and down another hall to find her door. I knock.

I hear movement on the other side, she opens, she's backlit.

"Come on in," she says.

I step inside. My eyes adjust and I see her for the first time.

It's the girl from the pics, but she ain't rosy-cheeked next to a dolphin. This chick's rail thin, scabbed-up face, pissy skin. It's like she's been on a year-long meth bender. She looks like the Holocaust.

She says, "I see you found it okay. Safe and sound."

"Yeah," I say.

I breathe in. It smells like stale smoke and failure.

I look around. It's a studio apartment. The only furniture she has is a bed and lamp. The lamp's not on. The overhead light is. It's fluorescent and flickering. Fast-food wrappers and pizza boxes are everywhere. There's a pile of clothes and mismatched shoes in the middle of the floor; next to that is a half-empty bottle of Coke with cigarette butts in it.

I look over at the bed. There's a piled-up pink comforter hanging off it, no sheets, and at the head of it, laying on the pillow, there's a warm bottle of orange juice.

She says, "You got here in no time."

I stop looking at the juice and glance back at her. It's like I'm 'bout to fuck Gollum.

"Yeah, I called a car…" I say.

"Get comfy," she says as she's shutting the door and locking the dead bolt.

I take another step in. I see on the other side of the room the closet door is cracked open. I wonder if her boyfriend's in there waiting to slice me with a box cutter. This is bad, I'm either gonna get robbed or get AIDS from this one.

She locks the dead bolt and I get a bump of adrenaline. I'm staring at the lock thinking 'bout getting kidnapped by meth heads, tied up in the tub, and being burnt with cigarettes.

My heart starts pounding.

I say, "Excuse me a sec…I just gotta do this one thing…"

I undo the bolt and leave.

She says, "Come back."

I walk down the hall in a controlled march, I hit the steps and try to calm down. I mean that was weird but I shouldn't be freaking out this much.

I get outside and take a deep breath of the night air. My face is flushed and my head's throbbing. My stomach feels like I've been drinking battery acid.

What the fuck is going on? I feel heat between my legs and it hits me, the bootleg Viagra's kicked in. It's not mixing well with the GHB. I prolly shouldn't have taken both pills. I shuffle down the hill towards Sunset with half a hard-on.

The more I walk, the more my dick rubs against my khakis and the more it rubs, the harder it gets. I'm full-blown erect by the time I pass a couple on their evening stroll.

I see 'em under the street light, they're Silver Lake's finest. He's a weak-chinned, bearded guy with a big-brimmed hat, she's wearing paint-splattered jeans, proof she's an artist. He's got her walking on the outside, like a bitch. I'm coming down the hill at 'em from the dark, in a red-faced stagger. I'm hunchbacked trying to hide this boner in my pants.

I see 'em tense up.

So I speak, "How you doing tonight?"

They pretend not to hear me.

I pretend not to be offended and continue on my way.

I make it to the main strip. Cars are whizzing by. I'm burping up Mexican food thinking about how that white chick with a dolphin was too good to be true.

Them OC bitches ain't gonna call me for a hookup. I'm leaning on a tree, puking up tacos in front of Intelligentsia. *Not the sober ones, at least.*

happy endings

DEON'S BOXING MY HEAD. Donnie's hyping him up, Yata's laughing with the rest of 'em.

We're in the grass on the side of my building. I'm swinging back. But I'm younger and smaller, it ain't doing much. I'm surrounded and eating punches.

He's bouncing around catching me. He's toying with me now.

I was just hanging out with these kids. They're my friends. But now we're fighting and I don't know why.

I thought we were friends.

At seven you don't notice, but we're a lot alike. We're all poor from broken homes.

Deon's dad's a drunk; so is Yata's.

Donnie's dad's in prison. He's never been around. All he has is one picture of him, from visitation. Donnie's next to him sitting at a metal picnic table, wearing a ball cap, smiling.

The first time I saw the pic, I got sad for him. His mom doesn't work. She's always doing her makeup but ain't never going nowhere. She just chain-smokes her Moores and waits for the check to come.

Deon's tired. I am too. There's a lull in my beating. It doesn't even hurt. I just feel left out and confused. I'm trying to talk to them, figure out how we even got here.

My hippie mom's got me living here, but she didn't tell me about not letting no one punk you, that "whys" don't matter when someone's punching you in the head, you just gotta make 'em stop.

They don't talk about that in my *Free to Be... You and Me* book. They just tell you to be nice. They don't tell you what to do when the other guy isn't.

I'm twirling my hair. My voice is high, it's squeaky, I sound like a girl. What'd I do? Why don't they like me? Can't we go back to fifteen minutes ago and be friends again?

I'm trying to reason with them, but kids don't understand reason. All they understand is force and candy.

They're letting me speak and I'm the center of attention, the way a calf surrounded by lions is.

Donnie's tired of hearing me talk. He tells Deon to hit me. So he does. And we're back at it.

What do I do?

My mom's people never taught me to fight. They're civil. They discourage violence. They have pleasant parties with good conversation and spinach dip. They never raise their voices. They don't disagree.

When I fight with my cousin or get loud at the dinner table and they see my dad in me, they don't get mad. They just avert their eyes and change the subject. And I finish my supper next to them, alone.

The kids are yelling, Deon's peppering my face, and my punches aren't working.

How would my dad handle this? He's wild. He can fight. He can whoop all their daddies.

It comes to me what he told me.

He squatted down in front of me and said, "If anyone fucks witcha, punch 'em in the fuckin' dick. Ya grab 'em by their balls and yank 'em."

In the moment this seems like sound advice. So that's what I do. I bend down and start swinging at his dick.

Deon's like, "What the fuck you doing?!"

I don't answer, I stay charging him. He backpeddles and punches my head.

I'm socking where his dick's s'posed to be, but it's not slowing this guy down. I'ma have to turn it up a notch. I'ma have to crush his balls.

He's lighting up the top of my head. I grab at his Lee jeans. They're tight. It's hard to grip. There's nothing there.

I guess ten-year-olds don't have a lot of dick.

The kids are yelling, "Ewwww, he gay!!"

"Jude a faggot!"

I won't quit. I just keep eating punches. He's hammer-fisting my back, the kids are yelling "fag" and I'm still grasping at his jeans. It looks like I lost a contact in his crotch and I'm trying to find it.

Frustrated, I finally let go of his Lees and Deon stops punching me.

I'm tired. I'm bent over breathing hard, looking down at his shoes. They're the Pumas with fat laces. Man, those are cool.

Donnie yells, "Jude, you gay as fuck!"

I look up, "No I ain't!"

Yata cracks, "Aaaaah you like dick, nigga."

They all laugh.

Deon's stuttering, "He wah-was all on my nutsack. Like a la-li'l fag."

Now I'm copping pleas. "No I wasn't! I was just trying to crush your balls."

"What?! Crush his balls?! Yeah riiight!"

They're howling. I'm embarrassed.

I'm still trying to explain myself when Deon steps up and pushes me in my chest. I flip backwards, over a kid bent down behind me, and land on my back.

Ooof!

I'm lying in the grass. My eyes tear up. Oldest trick in the book.

They leave me there and ramble off.

I crawl to my feet and look to see who snuck up and tripped me.

I shake my head. It was Trevor, the dirty-ass heavy metal kid.

Man, I forgot he was even there.

night moves

CRAIG DIDN'T WANNA PARTY, he just wanted something low-key. And that's what it looked like when we got there; seven people sitting in a semicircle, having quiet conversation, no music, CNN on with the sound off. They're covering Trump.

It's hot in here; it's cool outside. I go outside. I'm on my phone texting people not to show.

I'm coming down off the GHB, I take another pull from the bottle in my pocket.

I've been high all day. Me and Eddie, getting fried taking G walking down Sunset. Just a couple old dudes, checking out young chicks in their high-waisted short shorts, asses hanging out. They tug 'em down when we look at 'em.

I say under my breath, "You better. I'm a wolf, I'll eat you."

We hit some English pub in Echo Park for fish and chips. The food's mediocre. The prices are high.

The hipster Asian waitress asks us how we like it. I tell her I don't. She nods and smiles and walks away.

I'm chewing on this dry-ass Yorkshire pudding, I say, "Fuck she ask me for? She don't want the truth, she just wants a tip."

Eddie pops a fry. "They never do."

This little Mexican chick clears the table. We've been talking to her all night. She's a neighborhood girl with a chola accent and a can-do attitude, been bussing here since they opened and still ain't got bumped up to waitress.

That's how they do. Move in, take your shit, and hire the natives to do the grunt work.

It's got me thinking of this old-ass picture I saw today. Some spot gets colonized and this British motherfucker has this little brown lady carry him around in a basket strapped to her back. He's got on a safari hat, smoking a pipe, and she's happy to do it.

That's life. I slide the chola a ten and we leave.

I'm at the party on the deck waiting for the G to kick in. Eddie comes out with Craig and says he wants a hit. I hand him the bottle. I'm trying to think what we can use to measure it. This batch is strong; he probably only needs a half a teaspoon.

Before I can say anything, Craig opens the bottle and takes a monster swig.

My eyes go wide. He hands the bottle back. It's lost some weight. I hold it up to the light; it's halfway gone.

I'm like, "Um, Craig, you need to go throw up."

He says, "It's the same amount I did last time."

I say, "No, it's not. You did a bunch man, go 'url."

He rolls his eyes. "Dude, I'm fine."

I give him a look. When the druggy of the party is telling you to go puke, you should listen.

Eddie shrugs.

I'm like, "Don't say nothing when you wake up with a bloody asshole and a crumpled twenty in your hand."

I remind myself to leave early before the shit hits the fan.

Then the pizza shows up and my buzz kicks in.

Rob turns on some music. It's U2. Bono gets on my nerves, smug as fuck with his indoor sunglasses, but Rob's from Ireland so he's gotta like 'em the same way I gotta like Bob Seger.

I take a bite out my pizza and drink some Coke. I'm thinking, *This party's turning out pretty good.* Craig prolly didn't drink that much G. I've been going hard all week. I'm prolly just trippin'. New Order's playing. It's like being back at the roller rink.

I'm talking to Rob's girl about animal rights. I tell her, "They got the right to be my food."

She don't wanna hear that, but I'm an upper-middle-class American, I'm okay with being the top of the food chain.

She changes the subject to something we can both agree on: now we're talking about how much we hate vegans.

I look over and see Craig on the couch, leaning to the side, chin resting in his palm, mouth open. He's got a flop sweat going. I stay talking to her but I'm watching him. Now we're talking about gluten-free diets.

I'm halfway listening. "Uh-huh, uh-huh."

Then Craig's head drops forward like he's been shot, his chin hits his chest and his hand's still pointing up. I excuse myself.

I walk to the couch and bend over in front of him. "Craig, what up man? You good?"

Nothing.

I shake him a bit. He flops around. *Weekend at Bernie's.* I smack his cheek. Nothing.

Rob's girl comes over. "Is he okay?"

"Yeah, he just had too much GHB."

"What's that?"

I say, "The date-rape drug."

She says, "Oh."

She looks worried.

I'm trying to downplay it, "We could probably rape the shit out of him right now."

She doesn't laugh. She touches his forehead. "He's burning up."

"He'll be good," I tell her. "Prolly just sleep for an hour or two and wake up real horny."

It's happened to me a few times and that's how it ended, but I don't know about Craig. I don't know how much he did or how much booze he drank already. I'm thumbing the bottle in my pocket; goddamn it feels light.

I start thinking about this shit I read, some forty-year-old broad in Venice died off the G. Four people sent me the article this morning. She ODed at a beach rave. But I don't know how much she did, they never tell you how much they do. How you s'posed to not OD if they don't tell you how much?

People keep showing up to the party to find the birthday boy wrecked on the couch and I'm having to explain why. I wanna make sure I show concern but distance myself at the same time.

I'm shaking my head, shrugging, "I told him he drank too much, but he ain't wanna listen."

"Sure, Jude," they say.

It's an hour later, he's still not moving. We got the icepacks on him. I got a metal ice bucket in front of his face, waiting for him to puke.

Janet comes in from outside and says, "Is my friend gonna be okay…" she's holding up her phone, "…or do I need to call an ambulance?"

That's the last thing we need is some motherfucker in a uniform showing up.

I say, "He's fine."

She's says, "He doesn't look it."

I pretend to check his pulse. "Don't call nobody. He's good."

She takes a sip of wine and snaps, "Well, he better be."

I'm thinking, *If this guys dies, she's gonna be the one who tells on me.*

An hour later and he's still not up. Strangers are talking in hushed tones, whispering behind Solo cups. I can feel their eyes on me.

What if he don't make it?

I'ma have to find another house to stash my drugs. Rachel won't do it, Andrea neither. Ross has a kid. I'll dig a hole somewhere.

I look down at Craig; now he's convulsing. I'm really mad at this dude. Messing up the pizza party. He ain't listen, now we're here and I'm holding the bucket. This motherfucker better not die.

He stops moving. We sit in silence for five minutes, watching. Then he leans forward, opens his mouth, and wretches. He fills up the bucket. I empty it in the toilet and he fills it some more.

I'm holding it in front of his face, patting his back. "That's right, buddy. Get it out, man. Get it out."

He's puking and mumbling and I ain't never been this happy to see chewed-up pizza before.

brain games

THE RADIO JOB HAS me move to New York.

I get there in '04; it's a shadow of itself. Their pussies still hurt off the 9/11 shit and they ain't do nothing significant since the nineties. Worst part is, they been reading their own press so long, no one noticed the city turned into a fucking shopping mall.

I feel like a redneck in Manhattan. The cabbies hear my accent and try to take me the long way home. I'm always arguing with 'em.

I don't know where the good pizza is.

I ain't got no friends. All I have is work acquaintances and chicks I'm about to fuck or chicks I used to fuck.

New York is hard on me.

Work's even tougher.

I don't get along with the people at my job—all that keeping-it-real hood shit is bad for you in a corporate environment. I thought you could just check someone in hallway when they're fucking up. That's frowned upon, nowadays you need emails and paper trails. Talking nice is more important than being competent and nobody likes me.

My roommate's some Jewish broad that wears UGG boots and has Oscar parties with catty gay dudes that talk about celebrities' evening gowns. They never like 'em.

The only conversation I remember us having is her trying to sell me on Green Day's *American Idiot* album.

She hits a joint and puts it on. The lead dude's vocals sound like he used to get his lunch money took at school, then go home and get fucked by his uncle.

I'm staring at the stereo, I look up, "Is he always this whiny?"

She's got her eyes closed, humming along. "Shhhh. Just listen to the lyrics."

I sit quiet for like thirty seconds. Thinking about what I'm gonna do tomorrow.

I say, "Well, I like that, 'Hope you have the time of your life' shit they do, so…you know…"

I get up and go to my room. She stays and finishes the CD. I can hear it through the wall.

A few days later I'm out with Jessica, this little white girl I met through Annie. They know each other from rehab. They both liked coke too much and Jess was a cutter.

Jessica was looking for someone to choke her out, Annie said I could help.

It's Sunday night and Jess and I are trying to grab a bottle of pinot, take it home, and chill. Everything's closed. We walk all over the damn city and come back to my crib empty-handed.

The Jewish chick's entertaining in the living room. It's three couples. They're playing board games, laughing, and drinking wine. They stop when we walk in.

Jewish broad's fake polite and asks, "So, how's your night so far?"

I say, "Crazy, we just spent the last hour and a half looking for a bottle of wine. I guess everything closes early on Sundays out here."

She's nodding, glass of red in her hand, "Wow. Crazy."

I say, "Yeah…all we wanted was some wine."

They got three bottles of Merlot on the coffee table next to the game. The girl on the couch lifts her glass and takes a sip of hers.

I say, "That looks fun, whachall doing?"

Jewish chick's like, "Oh, you know, just hanging out and stuff."

I say, "Cool. What game is that?"

She says, "Cranium."

And that's it. There's room on the couch, but they don't scoot over.

They're looking up at us like when the waiter tells you what the specials are, nodding and smiling, waiting for us to go.

We're nodding now too.

The Jewish chick shrugs, "Whelp...looks like we better get back to the game."

I smile, point to my bedroom door, right next to the couch and say, "Well, I guess we're gonna have our own party in here then."

They raise their glasses and say goodbye.

We go in my room. They go back to laughing again.

I push my bed up against the shared wall, strip Jessica, and lay her on it. I put on some UGK and get naked too.

We don't do foreplay in rape sex. I spit on my dick and shove it in. I fuck her hard to gangsta rap. I choke her. I smack her face. I pull her hair. I'm gagging her mouth, fucking her doggy style, banging her face against the plaster when she finally comes.

We fall out on the bed. She's trembling and I'm out of breath.

I cut the music.

I don't hear them in the next room talking anymore. I don't hear 'em laughing either. Lights are out. Everybody's gone home. I guess they're done with their little game. Too bad, seemed like a nice party.

rocky

QUAN IS BOO'S FRIEND and Boo's my boy so that puts Quan around me. He's a year younger than us but more grown. He's built like a man and fucking women who could buy him beer.

His mom keeps him dressed fresh in Used jeans and Filas. He's always got the new shit. I'm impressed. I'm the dirt kid with two shirts that I switch off every other day.

His brother's locked up for murder. They said some kid stole his dope so he blew his face off with a shotgun. I don't know if that's true and if you ask Quan about it, he'll fight you.

We all hang at Boo's. Boo's dad's never home. He's gay and shacked up with his boyfriend in Warren. He leaves Boo there for days with a pack of hot dogs and a box of cereal.

We go nuts. It's blunts, video games, and fucking, listening to Troop and shit. Boo has everybody over, we run through his food in a day or two, then the neighbors feed him. Sometimes he asks my mom for something to eat and we give him some potatoes.

We ain't had shit either.

Quan don't like me. He never says nothing but I can tell. I don't bring it up, 'cause Quan's mean and I'm just glad he's not mean to me.

One time, we're all walking to the store and see some white boy riding a ten-speed down the sidewalk. I had never seen him before. He was listening to a Walkman, in his own world, riding real slow.

Quan says, "Ay, peep this." He starts jogging to the white boy. "Ay man, lemme holler atchoo right quick!"

The white boy stops peddling. He's standing there with the bike between his legs, lifting his headphones off his ears, waiting to answer a question.

Quan starts skipping to him, gets right near him, pulls back his fist and fires on him dead in his face.

The white boy flies off his bike and falls in the ditch. His Walkman's broke on the sidewalk. Quan bends down, picks up his bike, lifts it over his head, and throws it down on top of him. Calls him a bitch and jogs back across the street laughing.

Everybody starts cracking up, clapping their hands and pointing. They're yelling, "Hell nah! Y'all see that shit?! You wild, boy!"

They're all joking about the white boy, how dumb he looked with his headphones spun on his face. I look back and see him crawling out the ditch, blood leaking from his nose, confused. He's on his knees trying to collect his things.

It ain't funny, but I fake a laugh and keep walking. We don't see him around no more.

We hit 7-Eleven, Quan pulls out a knot and gets everybody Slurpees. I get cola mixed with red. He buys me off for a Slurpee. They're eating Better Made Hot chips, talking 'bout fuckin' hoes. I'm not saying much, I'm just chewing my straw.

We're walking back and see my boy Carlo's little brother Lanzo's at the playground with his Ninja Turtles. He's our age, but he's retarded so he still likes toys.

Quan sees him and stops. He picks up a rock from the ground and flings it at him. He misses. Lanzo's in his own world and doesn't notice.

We're all watching him play.

Quan picks up another rock and rubs it with his thumb, staring at him he says, "Goddamn, that's an ugly motherfucker."

I say, "That's Lanzo."

He says, "That nigga's head's big as fuck. He look like Mexican Rocky Dennis."

They laugh at that one. Then Quan throws his rock. He hits him this time. Lanzo looks up mad, he shakes his fist and lets out an, "Arrrrrr!"

Quan hears it and starts dying, grabs another stone and hits him again. He's got his hands on his knees, laughing. Mocking him, "Arararararara!"

The rest of the kids are laughing too. Now they're throwing stones. The more they hit Lanzo, the more he hollers. And the more he hollers the more they laugh. And it's funny but not funny.

I don't know if Quan knows Carlo, but I know some of the other guys do and they're still throwing shit at his retarded brother. I wanna say something. I wanna tell them to stop. But I don't. I just stand in the back and watch and wait for 'em to finish.

They're fucking him up. Lanzo's not mad anymore, he's scared and he's crying. He's trying pick up his toys and he keeps getting hit. I wish he'd just leave his toys and go. But he doesn't and they don't stop.

Then a car comes screeching up and slams on the breaks. It's Lanzo's mama, she's pissed. She yells out the window, "What the fuck are you doing to my kid!?"

Lanzo runs off to his house crying. His mom's cussing us out, standing in the parking lot with her car door open.

A few kids bail but most of us just stay and take it. She's really giving us the business. "Tuff guys, huh? Throwing rocks at a handicap? You little assholes better leave him alone!" Then she sees me in the back and points me out, "...and Jude, you should know better!"

I grew up with her kids. I've been in her home. I've eaten her food.

I look down ashamed.

"And you too, Boo! Don't try to hide, I see you! I should tell your moms! Punk motherfuckers! If you try that shit again, I'll beat your ass myself!" Then she spits on the ground, gets back in her car and tears off.

We watch her go and stand there in silence.

Quan's unfazed. He smacks his lips, "Goddamn she had a fat-ass booty." He looks at Boo. "You see all that ass? You wouldn't know what to do with that shit. I'd fuck the shit outta her."

Boo's like, "You should see her daughter, she look good too."

He says, "I don't know, but she need to stop all that talking and give a nigga some guts."

We all nod and agree. Then go back to Boo's to play Nintendo.

the velveteen rabbit

I MET EMILY AT a redneck house party in Flint. They had a bonfire in the backyard, they're drinking Natty Ice and listening to Pearl Jam.

She's smoking a square next to the cooler by a truck. I walk up on her and introduce myself. She's a white girl with a face like a china doll and eyes like a Husky. We lock in, I'm smitten, her shits are bluer than mine.

I ask her for a light. I'm smoking a clove.

She can smell it, she comments, "Are you smoking a clove?"

I tell her, "Yeah, I'm goth."

The rest of the night, I'm on her. She's got me open. We discuss the shit twenty-year-olds talk about before life whoops your ass, when you still got hope. We talk about the kabbalah, positive affirmations, and sun signs.

And, "Have you read *The Alchemist* yet?"

"Yeah sure. The gold was there under the tree the whole time..."

I get her beeper number before she leaves. We don't even kiss, we just hold each other and breathe. I fall into her eyes. My head's buzzing, I tell her.

She says, "That's your crown chakra."

I whisper, "I know."

It spreads all over my body and now we're vibrating. I want it to last forever.

It doesn't.

She's got a staff meeting at Hot Topic in the morning. She's gotta go.

I put her in her Dodge Omni and watch her tail lights shrink as she drives away.

I hit my clove and blow out the smoke. That chick is magic.

We talk on the phone a bunch, it's deep. We hang out when we can. It's dope. I'm taking my time with this one.

I even meet her and her family at the Renaissance Festival. She's wearing fairy wings, we hold hands. I get her a blown-glass wand. I buy her mamma a pickle.

It's all going good and then my truck breaks down and it's harder to drive that forty miles to go see her. She gets busy and can't chat on the phone as much. Then she starts fucking with this Mexican dude and we don't talk anymore.

I hear from Emily every now and again, mostly when she's having problems.

The Mexican cat she's fucking with beats her; she's telling me about it on the phone when he hops on. Now we're going at it and I'm on the phone arguing with this dude while my daughter's on the floor watching *Sesame Street*.

My kid's tugging on my jeans, wanting me to read her a book. I shake her off, "Not now, Assia. Daddy's busy."

I'm barking into the receiver, telling him real men don't beat on women.

We argue some more and I hang up feeling like a hero. She just needs someone that's gonna appreciate her.

I hit her up the next day to see how she is. Nothing. It takes a year before she calls me again.

I don't hold a grudge. When we talk, we're right back in it. It's deep, just like old times, except I gotta car that runs and she's single. Maybe we can make a go of it.

We make plans to catch up over drinks. The big night comes and she blows me off.

Emergency, no biggie.

Let's try another time. She blows me off again.

I'm sitting in that booth at TGI Friday's, waiting for her to show. I've got the waitress's sympathy and that feels worse than being stood up.

I'm looking at my life, like, *Wow, Jude, you on some real bitch-shit.* This don't happen to me, I dog hoes. This the second time she played me and I'm over here acting like if I love her hard enough, I'll get her.

I finish my water and tip the waitress. I thought she was the one. I guess I was wrong.

That's what I get for trying to save hoes. She don't wanna be saved.

A week later, she hits me with sorrys. I don't call her back.

Time goes by. I move down to 8 Mile. I start doing my little guest spot on TV and pulling way more chicks than I used to working third shift at the factory.

We're at the Pennzoil in my old neighborhood. Rachel's gotta get an oil change before she takes me to the airport; I'm going to Chicago, I'm doing *The Jenny Jones Show* tomorrow.

She's in the bathroom. I'm in the passenger seat of her car, zoning out to Portishead and there's a knock on my window.

I look up and some chubby Mexican dude's standing there, staring at me. He's smiling and nodding like he knows something I don't.

He says, "Ay, you Rude Jude?"

I say, "Yeah, that's me."

He grins. "I been waiting my whole life for this moment."

I'm thinking, *It's prolly some kid from the neighborhood that wants an autograph or something.*

I'm nodding, "That's cool man, you want an autograph or something? Hold up."

I start looking for a pen.

He says, "Nah, fool. I don't want your fucking autograph."

I stop looking for the pen. I look up and he's mean-mugging.

I say, "Well, whatchoo want then?"

He's rubbing his palms together by his chin.

He goes, "I'ma say one person's name and you'll know what I want." He pauses for effect, then he drops it on me with authority. He says, "Emily."

I look at him blank. I'm searching.

He's still rubbing his hands like a super villain, waiting for my reaction.

I got nothing.

I say, "Emily?"

He nods.

The week before, I got head from this redbone named Emily with TMJ. She blew me in the Hyundai and all I could hear was clicking. Maybe it's her.

I say, "Light-skinned Emily from Commerce?"

He shakes his head, "Nah, try again."

I'm thinking of all the different Emilys I've fucked with.

"She a raver?"

He says, "What? Nah, she's not a raver."

"Hrrm."

I'm racking my brain. Now I'm actually curious who this chubby Mexican is and what the fuck Emily he's talking about.

There was Emily from Pontiac. I talked her out of her virginity and then blew her off. She was sore about that, but that was years ago. Maybe this is her cousin or something.

I say, "Pontiac Emily?"

Now he's annoyed. "Nah, dog."

I say, "Well, you gotta help me out, man. Where she from?"

He says, "Emily Jansky."

I'm like, "Who?"

"Emily from Flint. I'm her boyfriend. Mike."

And then it all comes together. It seems like a lifetime ago.

I'm nodding slowly. "Oooooh. Alright, that Emily… Whatchoo doing in Auburn Hills, Mike?"

He says, real tough, "Selling magazine subscriptions."

I look behind him and there's a minivan with his coworkers watching, waiting for him to punk me.

I ask, "Like door-to-door?"

I'm thinking about how many magazines a motherfucker's gotta move to make a living at it.

He snaps, "Don't worry about it, bitch! Just stay away from my Emily."

I'm shaking my head, "Dog, I ain't seen her in forever."

He's like, "You fuck her?"

I tell him, "Ask your girl."

He's all worked up. "You fuck her, bro?!"

I smile. "Trust me, you're fine."

Now he's wagging his fat finger at me. "If you ever talk to her again, it's gonna be me and you. You hear me?!"

I look him dead in his eyes, he wants to fight now. I'm thinking I just gotta catch this flight and go to work.

I say, "Sure, Mike, whatever."

He stares me down, then turns around and walks away. He's nodding to the minivan. They're smiling like he just did something.

Rachel gets back in the car and asks what that was all about.

I say, "I just got fired from a job I quit a year ago."

big shot

I GOT TONS OF needles. My millionaire porn homie hooked me up with 'em.

I gave him some of my science drugs, in return he gave me this shit you shoot into your belly at night and you wake up tan. I don't even know what it's called, but I dig it 'cause I'm pink as hell, and that being pale shit went out in the 1800s.

I got the hypodermic in one hand and the phone in the other. I've been on the Internet for ten minutes trying to find the proper dose of K to shoot for a man my size. I usually blow lines, I'm not really into needles, but on a fluke I got this liquid shit.

I was on my way to buy some cologne and hit my job when my GHB connect accidentally shoots me a text about getting coke.

I hit him back—I don't want coke but I could use some ketamine.

He says he knows a guy and I end up deep in the North Valley for a deal.

We're in the parking lot of some shitty diner, sun beating down on us, making small talk next to his Yaris.

Waiting for his man.

My G guy's a bodybuilder, muscly as hell in a tank top, arched eyebrows and zits on his shoulders.

He's telling me about lifting. I'm barely listening.

Then he tells me he's quitting G. That gets my attention.

He says it's making him depressed.

I say I'm happy for him, 'cause that's what you're s'posed to say when people quit drugs. But now I'm worried about where I'ma get my next batch from.

His guy shows up in a Chevy Tahoe and parks on the far side of the lot. I give my G guy a stack of hundreds. He runs to the truck, hops in, and comes out a minute later with a paper sack. He hands it off to me and he's gone.

I never even see his connect. All I saw was sunglasses.

I throw my shit in the trunk, jump in the car, and I'm in traffic.

I'm giddy. I can't wait to be home. I'm on the on-ramp, behind this slow-ass Prius with a duct-taped bumper and a faded Obama "HOPE" sticker on the back, looking hopeless.

I'm thinking, *Goddamn, I left out this morning to buy some cologne and I end up with twenty vials of medical-grade ketamine in my trunk.*

I shake my head, pass the Prius, and turn up the Billy Joel.

I get home and call in sick. Then I bake two vials on a dinner plate, chop 'em up, and do rails till I puke.

I do a bunch the next day and throw up some more. At midnight I have a come-to-Jesus moment, take a Xanax and knock myself out. I wake up at nine feeling refreshed and I'm like, fuck Jesus, let's do it again.

Now it's nine thirty on a Sunday morning. I'm fried, trying to figure out how much ketamine I need to shoot to hit a K-hole.

I'm looking at the numbers on the side of the syringe, trying to figure out if they're milligrams or what? They didn't put no letters on this shit at all.

The numbers on the side go from zero to a hundred. I fill it to fifty. Fifty what? I don't know. I just figure it's a good compromise. I stick it in my leg and I'm thinking, *This is how motherfuckers kill themselves, 'cause twenty years ago they didn't pay attention in science class.*

I'm 'bout to push in the plunger when I get a call from an unknown number.

I pick up.

It's my daughter. We haven't spoken since our fight. She was fucking up in school, drinking too much. So I cut off her phone and drained her bank account. I shot her a couple emails since, but I never heard back.

This is our first time talking in months. I take the needle out of my leg.

We don't address the fight. She catches me up on her life. She got a job and switched majors.

I say, "Having your own money feels good, right?"

She says, "Yeah."

I tell her I'm proud of her.

She tells me she's chilled out with the partying.

I tell her be careful with all that drinking, she's got some wild ones in her family, that shit might run in her blood.

I tell her it doesn't matter what she majors in, if you're smart and humble and grind hard and be brave you can be anything you want.

I tell her to be brave.

I tell her I love her.

We get off the phone.

I think about her for a minute, in my apartment, in my new leather armchair. The sun's shining on my couch. A bird's singing outside my window. My drugs are on the ottoman in front of me.

I get up, I put on a Pharoah Sanders record, *Journey to the One*—it's sparse and moody.

I sit back down.

Pick up the needle and sink it in my thigh. I push the plunger in slowly and empty the syringe.

I listen to the sax play along with the sitar and wait for the K to kick in. I think about what I do. I think about what I'm doing to myself and why I keep doing it.

I might stop if I had a reason.

The song ends and I'm thinking maybe I should do some more. Because I still don't feel anything.

the sedona

NONNO BOUGHT THE VAN off this Persian motherfucker 'cause he looked like his little brother Pete, so he trusted him. He used to be good at buying cars. He's not anymore. He's old. He's old and he's worn down and Pete doesn't talk to him anymore.

He got the van 'cause Nonnie needed it to get around with her wheelchair. He moved her down to Florida, away from her family. He didn't wanna share her. When she was away from her kids, she died.

When we were little, Nonnie used to give us baths and send us home with spaghetti and meatballs. On Easter, she'd bake us rabbit-shaped cookies with eggs on their bellies.

When she was dying, I didn't go see her. We had a falling out over some family stuff. I called her instead, she told me she didn't wanna say goodbye so she said, "So long."

I said, "So long, Nonnie."

And that was it.

And I didn't feel much then, but it'll get me one day.

I think the casinos did her in as bad as the move to Florida did. The grandkids got big, we stopped coming around, so they'd go there. They were addicted to the slots.

They'd catch buses to Windsor and spend all day pushing that button, every day, a penny at a time, and show up late to Christmas.

Rachel used to get upset about it.

I'd shush her. "They're grown-ups, they can do what they wanna do."

But it's weird watching your grandparents turn into junkies. Her hand went bad from pressing the button and her body followed.

One time, me and Danny tried to meet 'em down at the Motor City Casino. We miss 'em by an hour and find a different busload of seniors. They're on the slots, in their sweatpants, with their walkers and oxygen tanks, being babysat by some black lady smoking a cigarette. Some of 'em pissed themselves. You can smell it. They don't care. They sit in it. They're still playing.

We never tried to meet 'em at the casino again.

That was a long time ago.

Nonnie's been gone awhile now. Nonno's in Florida alone.

His place is in shambles. He eats ramen noodles and sleeps in a chair. His van's broke down 'cause the Persian sold him a piece of shit.

He's in the driveway trying to fix it.

He used to wrench on cars, he used to build things. He's in his nineties now: his hands don't work like they used to.

He's got the battery out, it's on the ground. He's going in and out of the garage, getting tools when he trips and he falls and he breaks his neck.

And a month later he's dead.

I didn't see him to say goodbye either. He asked to see Rachel; he didn't ask about me.

the knockout

SHE HITS ME AND says she's never heard my radio show, she just knows me from the Internet and likes my jokes. She's quite fuckable, so I hit her back.

She lives near my daughter, in Florida. I'm gonna go see the kid next week.

I say, "Maybe we can arrange something when I'm out there."

She says sure.

First time I call her, she's says, "You don't sound how you look."

I say, "Yeah, I get that a lot. When I'm Internet dating, I gotta tell these chicks ahead of time that I sound black on the phone or they think they're getting catfished and freak out."

It's the truth and it usually gets a laugh, but it doesn't this time.

She says, "For sure, no one wants to get hit with a surprise nigger. Who wants to date one of those?"

Two minutes into talking to this chick and she's already dropping "surprise niggers" on me?

I pause.

I guess I'm s'posed to bring up the fact my daughter's half black and act morally superior. But that's an annoying person to be. I've met that chick before, she's the one who got knocked up by a black dude for culture and a cause.

I'm just trying to get my dick sucked.

I change the topic to something lighter.

Now she's name-dropping the celebrities she's slept with. It's only two. One's a midget. The other one's a comedian she fucked at his show. I know the guy. We're cool. She won't be the first chick I fuck after him.

It's almost like this chick's trying to talk me out of banging her. I don't know what's tackier, the racial slurs or her name dropping the B-list dicks that have been in her.

I don't wanna hear you talk about fucking other dudes unless I'm jerking off to it. As far as the "nigger" shit goes, I shrug it off. She's Bolivian and wasn't taught to mask her bigotry the way whites have been.

We make a date to hang out the night I get in. I'll fuck her, then meet up with my kid the next day.

I touch down and hit her. We're eating tacos at a table on the sidewalk. She's drinking a Corona, trash-talking the city.

My daughter lives here. I tell her, "I like it."

I take a sip of my G.

She says, "What's that?"

I say, "GHB."

She says, "Ooh, I love G. I haven't done that since Miami. Gimme."

I shake my head, "I don't know... I don't like giving chicks I haven't fucked yet 'the date rape drug.'"

She insists. "Come on..."

I pour her a cap. She drinks it and makes a face.

She says, "I think it's real cool of you to meet up with your fans."

I laugh. I say, "Girl, I drive a Mazda Six with cloth interior. I'm not above fucking girls off the Internet."

We eat our Mexican food and she puts down every single person that walks by us.

"Ew, he's fat... She's got an ugly butt... I know she didn't wear that..."

I'm quiet chewing my food. I don't laugh once.

I'm guessing there's a few things going on here. One: she's nervous. Two: I'm known for talking shit and she's trying to measure up. And three: this chick's a knockout and nobody tells her to shut the fuck up when she sounds like an idiot. So here we are.

Finally, I say, "You know, Maria... Why don't you just be nice?"

She says, "What?"

I say, "You shit on every single person that's passed us."

She says, "No I haven't."

I say, "Yeah, you have. Just be cool."

She looks down. She's quiet for a second, then takes a bite of her quesadilla, "Too much cheese. You must be excited to see your daughter tomorrow."

This'll be the first time I've seen her since our fight.

I say, "Yeah, I really am."

She says, "Aw, that's sweet. Do you have a picture of her?"

I take out my phone. I pull up a pic of her and her friends. I hand it to her.

She says, "Awwww, how cute!! Which one is she?"

I take a bite out my taco. I chew it up.

I say, "The black one."

We're back in my room. She's too faded to drive but not too faded to fuck. We'll smash for a while and I'll send her on her way.

I'm thinking, *Maybe I shouldn't have gave her that second cap of G when she bugged me for it.*

It kicked in at the bar when we were shooting pool, she kept smacking my ass, talkin' 'bout, "Ooh, you like that don't cha!? Don't cha!?"

And I'd be like, "Nope, actually, I don't."

And then she'd spank my ass again and strut away holding her pool cue like a scepter.

In bed she's doing the same shit: ripping off my belt and throwing it across the room. I wish she'd be careful with it, it's alligator. Now she's talking trashy about what she's gonna do to my dick; suck the shit out of it, she says.

This ain't even sexy. It's like she saw this scene in a porno and now she's doing it to me.

I'ma have to take control. I grab her, kiss her on the mouth. She's got soft lips. It's actually quite nice.

I'm undoing my pants, looking at her. She growls, smacks me across the face, and says, "Give it to me."

I sigh.

I take out my dick. She goes down on me with more enthusiasm than skill. Tugging and jerking with lots of teeth. She seems to like it, but I don't know how long I can deal with this wack-ass head.

You show me a guy that says, "There's no such thing as a bad blow job," and I'll show you a guy who never gets his dick sucked.

She looks up at me and says, "I love sucking your cock. You got me so hot right now."

I pull her panties aside and touch her pussy.

I say, "Your pussy's not. It's dry as hell."

She says, "Well get me wet then."

I put her on her back and go down on her.

I start slow then go fast. She's making noises. I'm trying to match strokes to moans. She's getting louder, saying my name. I find that pace and lock on. I throw a finger in her. She's wet and squeezing it. She's got good pussy for being a dick. This's gonna be fun. She's about to come with the high pitched *ohs*.

She tenses up. Releases and then she goes quiet.

I lick softer. I'm thinking, *Oh she wants to be still.* I'm lapping at her trying to get the post-nut shudders out of her, but she ain't moving. So I speed up the tongue, see if I can get her to yelp.

Still, nothing.

Hrrmm. That's odd.

I take my face from out of her vagina, raise up, and look. She's spread eagle and out cold. She drank too much G.

I shake her, call her name, slap her cheek. She's still out.

Goddamn it.

She ain't drunk enough for me to be scared, I'm just annoyed.

I'm thinking, *How you like that? She gets her nut then goes to sleep. Fucking lightweight.*

I'm kneeling above her holding my dick. She's knocked out, pouty lips, looking all peaceful with her legs open and that monkey glistening. I really wanna fuck.

She's actually quite stunning when she's not talking. I'm staring at that pussy, man it is wet. Ain't shit to do but one thing, I grab my pants off the floor, dig in my pocket, grab my phone and set the timer for two hours.

Let her sleep that shit off, I'll fuck her later. She'll prolly need to sober up before she drives home anyway.

I used to wake up my exes in the middle of the night with dick, that was sexy. This'd be date rape. I shut my eyes and take a nap.

Two hours come and go. She's still out. I'm thinking of all the shit I gotta do in the morning.

At three she finally wakes up. "What happened?"

I say, "You passed out while I was eating your pussy. Right after you came."

I had to tell her she came.

She gets up to get some water. I turn on the lights and see a giant oblong circle on the comforter where she was laying.

I touch it. It's wet.

I say, "Jesus Christ."

She says, "What?"

I say, "Goddamnit, Maria. Ya pissed the bed."

She yells, "Nooo!"

I'm staring at the stain. I'm not even mad. We're just not fucking now, for sure.

She says, "I think I'm gonna go."

I nod. I say, "Yeah, you better."

I walk her out and she's stumbling in her heels, she's still high. There's a fifty-fifty chance she's gonna wreck her car. If that happens, there's a fifty-fifty chance she'll tell on me. I don't like the odds but I'ma have to take 'em, 'cause the thought of waking up next to her is unbearable.

She's damn near falling over when I put her in her car and point her in the right direction.

I'm wired in bed next to her piss, it's cold, I can feel it. I'm in the dark, thinking about life decisions and what led me here.

I'm thinking, *You coulda took your kid to get tacos tonight, but you decided to fuck some chick you didn't even like.*

And for what? A nut? A notch? Get her to come so you could feel good about yourself? Fucking these hoes is like picking a lock and all you got is five moves.

Banging random hoes at twenty is cool; at forty it's pathetic.

I'm pinching the bridge of my nose. I say out loud to the room, "Oh, don't beat yourself up. You're not gonna stop till you settle down… But they're never good enough for you, are they? You just wanna smart girl. But the smart ones are too smart to fuck with your ass."

So here we are.

I jerk off in bed. This bitch is prolly wrecked somewhere. Telling the cops how I gave her drugs. Better stash that G just in case.

I'm looking around the room for a spot.

Don't be paranoid. You're good.

God, I'm exhausted. Just drink you some coffee tomorrow, go swoop your kid, you'll be good. You'll be good. Go to bed, man. You're good.

I'm finally dozing off and my phone chirps.

It's a text from Maria. I read it. It says, "omg I just got pulled over for speeding. omg fml." She ends it with a sad emoji face.

I sigh the day away. I put the phone on the bed stand and pretend like I never got that text.

last call

JULIE GETS THE FIRST copy of *Hyena* I write. So much of the book's about her, I want her to have it. Even the stories she's not in, all the chicks I fucked; I was thinking of her when I was doing it.

I reach out to her. She texts me an address. I mail her the book. A year later she calls me.

It's good to talk to her, just to hear her voice, to hear how she's doing. At first she's guarded but she warms up. An hour into it, I'm lying in bed talking, she's parked in her driveway but she doesn't wanna go yet.

Her voice has changed. It's softer and sweeter. It sounds like it used to when she loved me.

It's getting late. I ask, can call her the next day?

She says okay. She's done with work at nine.

Next day I'm giddy. I swore I was over her but I guess I'm not. It's funny, the lies we tell ourselves just to get by.

Maybe we can work it out. Maybe after everything, we can start over and have a storybook ending

Nine o'clock can't get here soon enough. I'm at the V-Cut playing backgammon, I can barely think. I'm getting my ass whooped but taking it as a good omen.

Like the old Armenians say, "Unlucky in dice, but lucky in love."

I'm driving home down Melrose bumping Supertramp—*Oh Darling, I'm gonna make you mine.* I'm singing along like they wrote it for me. And when it's over I bring it back again.

Nine o'clock comes, I play it cool. I wait till nine thirty to hit her.

No answer.

An hour goes by and I'm dying. I'm staring at my phone waiting for it to ring. The next hour's even worse. People keep texting. It's not her, and with every text my heart sinks a little more.

Probably just busy.

She finally hits back at midnight.

It's not the same Julie I hung up with the night before. This one's cold.

She says, "So what'd you want to talk about then?"

I should've said, "Nothing." But I gotta see it through.

I tell her I'm grown now. I'm more patient now. I been working on myself. I tell her back then I counted on her to make me happy and when she didn't, I resented her for it. I tell her I finally figured out I'm just not a happy dude.

She gives me a noncommittal, "Yeah."

I tell her I'm like an old house that she's done all these repairs on and it'd be a shame if she let someone else move in.

I say, "Maybe we can try again."

I ask her, does she wanna try again?

The line's quiet.

I probably shoulda just suggested coffee.

I'm in the dark, sitting on the edge of the bed, looking at shadows on the wall, waiting for an answer.

I say her name. Then she tells me she has a boyfriend.

"Oh," I say.

We're silent.

I ask her, "Why ain't you tell me you had a man yesterday?"

She says, "I didn't know when to bring it up."

I force a laugh, "Probably towards the beginning of the conversation."

"Yeah, I guess so," she says, "Hey Jude, it's late. I better go."

She hangs up.

I text her. If she ever needs anything, I got her. As soon as I send it, I regret it. So I hit her right back, "Never mind, I'ma leave you alone. Let you live your life."

She doesn't reply. Now I'm thinking, *Did that come out the wrong way?*

I start texting her another paragraph about how I meant the last text to mean that she should have good luck with her guy and her life and I'm happy for her.

I'm about to send this one off when I stop.

"You bitch," I say.

This is embarrassing. I erase it. I erase her texts. I erase her number. I try to forget it.

"She don't want you no more, you fuckin' weirdo."

I turn on a light and sit with that.

Me and my fairy tales.

She don't want you no more.

And this one hurts a lot, but not as bad as last time.

monster

I DRESS UP LIKE Jeffrey Dahmer for Halloween, but most people just think I'm a pedophile.

I'm walking down the boulevard with Taz, Zee, Toni, and Ross. Ross is the black Marty McFly, Toni's Amy Winehouse. Taz and Zee don't dress up but chicks still think Zee's Charles Manson.

It's a real shitshow in Santa Monica. We're eating hot dogs, looking at costumes. Everyone's wasted.

Some dyke pirate's sloppy drunk, crotch out on the concrete next to us. Her girls are trying to help her. They're all in our space. So we give 'em our table and offer them water.

They take it and don't thank us.

Tazzy smiles and says, "You're welcome."

The tranny looks up and notices their faux pas and goes, "Oh...thanks."

I force a smile. "Yeah, we're all in it together."

And they're back on their phones texting.

This ain't my first Halloween parade. It'll probably be my last. I remember the costumes being better.

It's getting late. Let's go home.

Ross drops me at the crib and I start doing rails of K.

I got chicks hitting me up to hang. I'm tunnel-vision muscling my way through the texts. I got a little Jewish girl s'posed to come over after the bar. I better try and sober up, but first lemme finish these lines.

At 1:30 a.m. the webcam girl hits me for a threesome. I cancel the Jew and eat two Viagras.

Half-hour later, I text Webcam, "Where you at?"

She's drunk. She doesn't know. She's at a party.

I say, "Still?"

I tell her screenshot the map.

She does. She's in Brentwood. In the hills. At least forty minutes out.

She's not coming.

I text her, "Great. You fuckin' asshole. You cock-blocked me from twenty miles away."

I try and uncancel the Jewish chick but it's too late, it's going straight to voicemail. I jerk off but I'm too high to nut, so I go to bed at four with a raging hard-on.

I wake up at seven, drink GHB, and go antiquing. It's slim pickings. All I find are a couple records: Brian Eno and Smokey Robinson. It's getting hot, so I go.

By eleven I'm at my boy's watching football and snorting ketamine. Sports are a waste on K. Just a bunch of dudes running around for nothing; pointing their fingers to God.

I sober up long enough to have dinner with the twenty-two-year-old vegan.

She's telling me about going to USC. Now they got these things called trigger warnings at her school. Like if you're about to show some shit with violence or rape in it, you gotta warn 'em ahead of time, so it doesn't *trigger* bad feelings or they'll freak out and get traumatized.

I say, "They do this for grown-ups?"

She says, "Yeah."

"They war vets or some shit?"

She says, "No."

I'm shaking my head. It's come to this? These are my future bosses.

No trigger warnings in life, just sharp corners. Shit happens then you deal with it.

I liked it better when we were cowboys and Vikings, taking people's shit. Now we're allergic to peanuts and a piece of bread'll kill ya.

I send her home; I've heard enough for the night.

Let's do some more ketamine.

I do more. I'm in a K-hole. I'm paranoid. I'm thinking, *I'm really Jeffrey Dahmer*, I'm thinking, *I'm dead.* Man, I could use some pussy. I'm arguing with myself. These clothes feel weird.

I come to an hour later, holding my phone, butt-naked with a sweater on. My dick's flaccid, my top's turquoise.

I'm embarrassed. I look down at my phone. Did I post this on the Internet? Did I send the vegan a dick pic?

I hope not, I was trying to be her mentor.

I need some pussy though. I'm on Backpage jerking off with coconut oil, looking for a hooker. I try to make an appointment but when she answers, I'm too high to form words.

I get a text from a woman I used to see. She's actually a grown-up with a career. I tried to date her but she wanted commitment without intimacy and I ain't know how to do that. Now we just fuck once in a while.

She wants to visit and I wanna eat her up. I tell her come over, the door's unlocked. Let yourself in.

I make a playlist.

She shows up a half-hour later. I go down on her to "Munchies For Your Love." It's fitting. We fuck until she's sore. We lay in bed and talk. It's nice, these quiet moments.

She wants to stay. I don't let her.

I send her home and my face is back in the plate.

I'm spun. I'm exhausted but I gotta keep going. There's more to do.

I remember going to a psychic for work a few years back.

She asks me what I wanna know.

I tell her, "Keep it light."

She starts off, "You're a writer."

I say, "Yeah, I am."

She says, "You got mental illness in your family."

I say, "Who doesn't?"

She says, "This is weird but just go with it."

I say, "Okay."

She says, "You have a demon stalking you. He's here with you right now, laughing."

I say, "Hell nah! A demon?"

She says, "Yes," and starts describing textbook examples of depression.

Then she says, "Someone in your family did something very evil to let these dark forces around you."

I tell her, "That's just depression. It runs on my pop's side."

She says, "It's a demon. What'd your father do?"

I'm looking at her like, *You're the psychic one, you tell me.*

I say, "Nothing."

She's shaking her head, "Hrmmm."

She doesn't believe me.

I get up to go. She gives me her card. She says she can fix me for more money. She says she does phoners.

I throw it in the trash.

I'm talking myself down. "It's just depression. I'm just depressed."

That's all it is, I've had it as long as I can remember. Gabby used to call it "my moods." Julie didn't call it anything, she just hated it.

I'd try to explain it to her. She ain't get it.

She'd say, "Why can't you just be *happy*? Why not choose *happy*?"

I'd say, "You think I chose this shit?" I tell her, "It's like I got a black stain on my heart and no matter how hard I scrub it, it's still there. And no matter how happy I am, it's gonna be there waiting for me when the joy goes away."

She'd just sip her wine and look at me like I was pathetic. And I'd stare back. Then she'd shake her head and we'd change the subject.

They say exercise helps with that shit, maybe I shoulda jogged more.

Now she's long gone and I'm blowing rails without her.

Nights like these, I think about what that psychic said. I think about that demon on my back with a riding crop. Whipping me. Driving me to finish that plate.

We all got demons. This one is mine.

I finally get to bed at four and wake up in the morning with a herpe on my lip.

Goddamn it, I went so hard I had a fucking outbreak.

These fucking herpes, I call 'em "Face AIDS." I got 'em from my aunt when I was nine and she kissed me goodbye with a cold sore on her mouth.

They come out when I'm stressed. I get 'em in my eyes too. They're my little reminder that no one can hurt you quite like your family.

I cancel all my dates for the week.

This ketamine'll keep me company. I drag ass through work then come home and do K. I do it till I'm sick and I'm puking and my brain's floating outside of my head.

I'm on the couch, burnt, thinking maybe I should chill. I wash the rest of the gram down the sink.

I reach out to my friends. I'll hang out with my friends instead.

I take G walks and have dinner. It's fine.

I'm off the K and the insomnia sets in. I'm spaced out during the day. I'm wired at night. I don't know how long I can do this for.

Five days off, I hit an art show in an attempt to be human. I even put on a tie.

I get there, it's a real scene. Everyone's pretty. They're all wearing the right clothes.

I'm solo. I try to mingle but feel disconnected and cats keep coming up with reasons to leave. I'm left there next to a picture, holding my water. I pivot.

I talk to women my age, they're all married and their husbands are there and they grab their wrists and lead them away.

Man, them dudes are tripping. It's just small talk, that's all it is.

But is it? I haven't touched a chick in a week. It's wearing on me. I haven't felt this needy in a while. I bet they can smell it.

Maybe I missed my window. Everyone's coupled up here. I'm the old guy at the bar, still single. A lecherous old man, hitting on women with a herpe on his lip. I used to laugh at that dude.

I'm on the sidewalk in a group; they're smoking weed. I end up standing next to some Filipino chick wearing blue contacts and a poncho. She looks like an alien but I talk to her anyway.

We're all in it together.

She tells me she's getting her doctorate in management at the University of Phoenix. That's the same one they have commercials for during *People's Court*.

I'm genuinely surprised. I say, "No shit? They got PhDs for managers?"

She rolls her eyes. "Yup, they sure do."

I say, "All my managers ever do is pass the buck."

She forces a "Ha."

I smile. I say, "Maybe they wouldn't if they had PhDs."

Now she's looking around for someone better to talk to.

I think she's into black guys.

I might be wrong, but she's got a way about her that feels like she'd blow a dude to a Mos Def album. She gives me her back and starts talking to a black dude wearing a cape.

I'm left there thinking, *I just got dissed by a bitch who goes to Internet college.*

I crack a smile. It's probably time to go home.

I call a car. I go home. I make an egg sandwich and eat it over the sink.

I dig through my cabinet; I know it's here somewhere. Then I find it, sitting behind the vitamin B: my last bag of ketamine.

rocky II

WE AIN'T HAVE SHIT to do that day. Just like every other day. We're sitting around Boo's eating microwaved hot dogs in folded-up white bread, watching TV on the black-and-white, switching between basketball and karate flicks, turning the channel with some pliers.

The phone rings. Boo tells me to be quiet, it might be his dad. It's not. It's Quan. He says to come outside in ten minutes.

We watch Bruce Lee till the commercial break then go sit on the porch.

Quan rolls up a half-hour later in an '82 Bonneville, bass bumping.

This is impressive. Quan might look like he's twenty, but he's really thirteen.

He parks diagonal in the lot and hops out with the music still blasting.

Boo runs over and gives him a pound. "Where you get this shit?! This your granddad's?"

Quan's like, "Hell nah, I got this off a crackhead. This a chronic-car."

Boo looks it over. "It's clean though."

Quan says, "Yeah, I got this bitch all day, while he's working. Let's go."

We run back in the house and put on our good clothes; I borrow a shirt from Boo and we bail.

It's pretty fun driving around. We pick up a couple more kids. We cop some beer from Hilltop. We roll through all the neighborhoods showing off. When the police get behind us, we turn down the music, everybody takes off their hats and acts cool.

We end up at the mall looking at shoes. They're hollering at girls; I'm shoplifting cassette singles. Security kicks us out and we're behind Mervyn's taking turns learning how to drive.

It's my turn. This my first time, I'm nervous and going real slow.

Quan's losing his patience. "Man, park the car, lemme show you."

I hop out. He gets behind the wheel and starts whipping it.

He's talking shit about how easy it is. "Man, you can't drive for shit. You drive the car, car don't drive you. Watch me."

He hits a couple donuts, tries to do another one but it's too tight and runs into a pole. We all get out and look at the damage. The front end's fucked.

Boo says, "That front end's fucked."

Quan shrugs. "Oh well."

We meet the chronic at the body shop. He's a nervous-looking white dude in his forties. He's rail thin with a mustache and glasses, wearing a beat-up Members Only jacket. He looks like he fucks children.

He's talking to Quan in the corner, shaking his head, muttering. "Jesus Christ, what the hell happened, Quan?"

"Dog jumped out and I swerved not to hit it and ended up in a pole."

The chronic's looking out the window at the busted-up car in the parking lot.

He sighs. "A dog, huh?"

Quan shrugs. "Yup."

We leave the dope fiend with his car and take a cab home.

We're back at Boo's house piled on his mattress watching TV again, bored.

Quan says, "Y'all wanna get some money?"

We're like, "Yeah."

He hits his Newport ashes into an old bowl of cereal and says, "Well, y'all got some money?"

Boo shakes his head, "I'm broke till my daddy get here."

Real proud, I say, "I got money."

I'm dirt poor. But this Christmas my Nonnie gave me fifty bucks.

It's a big deal, they're usually cheap. They're Italian immigrants from the depression. They steal napkins from McDonald's and take the bread home from restaurants.

The Christmas before, my sister got a broken typewriter and me and Danny got some dead Evereadys.

We're like, "Nonno, what we s'posed to do with these dead batteries?"

He says, "Build something."

So getting that fifty was like hitting the lotto. It's been sitting in my underwear drawer for two months while I figure out what I'm gonna do with it.

Quan asks, "How much money you got?"

I say, "Fifty bones. What we gotta do?"

He says, "I gotta spot on the west side, we can grab you a fifty-dollar double-up and turn it to a hun' in a couple hours."

I never sold crack before, but I didn't have shit else to do and a hundred bucks sounded pretty good.

I say, "Hold up, I'll be back."

I run home, grab the money out my drawer. My mom's cooking, she's like, "What are you up to tonight?"

"Just gonna hit the movies with Boo and 'em."

She says, "Well, have fun."

I say, "Okay. I love you." And I'm out the door.

We take a cab over to Clark and Oakland, hop out and walk over to a field by the railroad tracks. I cop from a fat black kid in a Bulls starter.

He eyeballs me, looks at Quan, and says, "Who's this?"

Quan's like, "That's my dog."

I'm thinking, *Yeah, I'm his dog.* I give him the money and get the rock. It's smaller than I thought it would be. We head to the spot to chop it up.

It's a halfway house turned dope-house filled with a bunch of old-ass ex-cons getting served by teenagers. We pass by this nappy-headed black motherfucker sitting on the steps. He's eating dog food out the can, he shit his pants. He's muttering.

Upstairs, the carpet's ratty, the linoleum's peeling, the walls are exposed. Quan gives some square-looking white dude a five-dollar pebble to let us use his bedroom. He's grateful. He stuffs it in a chopped-up radio antenna and smokes it.

We're at the dresser cutting up the rock with a razor blade and twisting the smaller pieces in saran wrap. I get ten out of it at ten a pop. I put 'em in my pocket.

"Now what I do?"

He says, "Just chill in here and serve these custos."

I post up in a lawn chair. I bullshit with Boo and wait for sales. The shit-stained black guy keeps staggering up and down the hallway, stinking up the place.

An hour goes by, nothing.

Selling crack is boring.

A dope fiend shows up with his crack-hoe girlfriend. He's a Waterford redneck with a moustache and mullet. She's light-skinned with delicate features.

I bet she was pretty once, but her hair's cooked, her skin's jaundiced, and her jeans don't fit.

Quan and a couple other dudes are in the redneck's ear working out a deal. Tricks are slow on Clark Street. She's rocking in the doorway, smoking a cigarette, waiting for them to figure it out.

The shortest one gives the redneck a rock, he nods to his girl. She takes off her windbreaker, grabs shorty's hand, and goes across the hall with him. They shut the door. The redneck splits and all the kids take turns fucking her for ten-dollar rocks.

They all get done and Quan says to me, "Take some dope and go get some guts, nigga."

I ain't hit puberty yet. I got a dick like a toddler. There's no way I'm taking that shit out in public. I try to play it off and sound cool.

"Nah, man, you know…I'm good… She look scurvy as hell anyway. Your dick prolly smell like tuna fish after that shit."

Quan says, "Fuck you talkin' 'bout my dick for?"

I say, "You know, 'cause her pussy stank…'cause she like a hoe…I ain't trying to get AIDS…"

"Nigga you sayin' I got AIDS?"

"Nah, man, I'm just sayin', I'm tight."

One of the other guys just stares at me then leaves.

Quan says, "Whatever, you scared."

He walks out and I'm stuck there serving. I'm thinking, *Wow, that was real corny of me.*

I end up selling three rocks in three hours. This is the slowest fast money ever. I shoulda brought my Game Boy.

I'm pacing the room. The air's stale and sour. The lighting's harsh, just a lamp with no shade and a TV with no sound.

Now the corny white dude's got me next to his bed and he's trying to trade me some Isotoner gloves for twenty dollars worth of dope.

He's got the gloves in my face talking 'bout Dan Marino. I look away and see, laying on his cinder block nightstand next to the ash tray, a school picture of a girl my age. She's got brown hair, she's pretty, she looks like him.

He's showing me the tags are still on. His kid got 'em for his birthday but they don't fit, he says. It'd be a shame for them to go to waste. He's damn near begging me. I'm thinking, *This selling dope shit is depressing.* I'm ready to go.

I tell Boo and Quan I'm leaving. Boo wants to roll too. We head downtown looking for a cab.

We're standing at the light and see Quan come running up. He's hollering. We walk over to him. Maybe he forgot something.

He's bouncing on the balls of his feet.

He says, "What up then!?"

We're confused, Boo's like, "We going home. What up?"

He looks at me, he says, "Nah, bitch. What up witchoo?! Heard you was talking shit!"

I say, "Whatchoo talking about, Quan?"

He don't say shit. He just hits me with a three-piece in my face and I go down. My head's rocked. My ears are ringing. I'm lying in the gravel.

I hear Boo yell, "What the fuck, man!? Chill out!"

I feel a kick in my head, then another one.

I hear Quan say, "Boo, if you don't let me go, I'ma fuck you up too."

Now I'm sitting up dazed, I got my eyes open. He's standing over me.

He says, "Get up and fight me, bitch."

I'm scared, I'm trying to reason with him. "I ain't got beef witchoo, Quan!"

He catches me with a looping right. "Shut the fuck up."

Boo's begging him to stop. "Quan, come on…"

I stand up. I'm dizzy and shook. I say, "Please, man…"

"Fight me, li'l bitch." He points to the ground. "For real, you not gonna fight me? There's a rock right there, hit me with that shit!"

I look down and there it is. I'm afraid if I bend down to get it, he's gonna catch me again. And I'm scared if I swing on him, he'll beat even me worse.

So I run. He gives chase.

He catches me and whoops my ass till he gets bored. Then walks back to the dope house.

I'm banged up in a cab driving home down Perry Street and I'm looking out the window. We talk about it for a while and try to figure out why. Then we both go quiet.

I'm thinking, *Getting kicked in the head hurts but not half as bad as going out like a bitch does. That takes years to get over.*

I find out later from Boo why he whooped me. The west side dudes were giving him a hard time for bringing a white boy around who wasn't a customer. So he beat me up to prove a point.

He did it for them and they didn't even come out and watch.

the odd couple

CHRISTINA KICKS THE JEWISH chick out of her New York apartment and moves back in. We get along great. We cook together, drink wine, do drugs, everything.

A year into it, Chris gets tired of my antics. My one-night stands, bringing drunk chicks home; they're tripping over furniture, being loud, giggling.

Next morning, she's gotta wake up to their shit in the living room and them pissing in the bathroom when she's gotta get ready for work.

She gives me the business.

I tell her, "I'ma chill out."

She says, "You better."

I say, "You got it."

That night I go out with Tino, this Croatian cat from the job. We're at some French spot eating mussels when I get a call from Kristy, this porn chick I met in Vegas.

She says she's in town for one night and needs a place to crash.

I say, "You can stay with me."

We meet up at a cigar bar in SoHo.

She looks how one might expect a porn chick to look in '06. Tight blue jeans, white leather jacket with the tassels everywhere, matching white boots with tassels too, fake tits, big hair, shitty highlights, and an orange-skinned fake tan.

She looks kinda like a slutty carrot.

We're barhopping. She's not drinking. I'm trying to loosen her up. She's actually pretty cool, but surprisingly uptight for a chick who gets sodomized on camera.

We end up at some Wall Street bar. Tino wants to go there 'cause he heard Jenna Bush is s'posed to show.

The place is my nightmare, it's a bunch of young Republicans, rich and cocky as fuck. They're doing tons of blow, sweating through their Polo shirts, waiting to get old enough to take over their dads' companies.

We lose Tino in the crowd, he's in the VIP dick-riding some celebrity. I'm standing at the bar with the porn chick.

We keep getting bumped and jostled, these bitches keep stepping on my shoes and not saying excuse me. They're awful people. I'm looking at Kristy, trying to apologize with my eyes.

I wanna make the best of it but when they all start singing "Sweet Caroline," I grab Kristy and leave. We're out the door by the time the second *da da da da*s hit.

We hit a dive bar in the LES for a nightcap. I'm on whiskey, she's on Sprite. We're bonding over how much we hate rich people. I think I got her beat.

She's shitting on my boy Tino, calling him a fake-ass starfucker.

She's kind of right but I don't got a lot of options out here.

I say, "Yeah, I guess so. But that's why he knows the good bars."

She rolls her eyes. "Whatever, good bars. That last club was filled with every kid I ever hated in high school."

I raise my glass to that. "Touché, li'l mama. Touché."

She's pleased with herself and I finally talk her into having a real drink with me. We do a shot and go home.

We're in the taxi when a switch flips. Her eyes glaze over; she's staring in the distance. We're driving blocks and blocks, she's not talking.

Something feels off and the silence is making me uncomfortable.

I try to fill it. "You see that shit out the window over there? That's a Picasso. He was the one that really got all that fucked-up-face-shit poppin'... You know, wit the ear on the cheek and shit?"

She doesn't answer.

I point at another building, "That's NYU. S'posed to be a good college."

She stares straight ahead and whispers, "Shut up."

I don't know if she's talking to me or the cabby. So I say, "What?"

She says, "Stop talking. Be quiet."

I'm thinking she got me fucked up. I say, "You got me fucked up. You better chill out 'fore you end up walking."

Dry as hell, she says, "Okay."

"Anyway that's NYU. That's where the rich kids go…"

Under her breath she mutters, "Shut up, bitch."

"Huh?"

"Shut your face."

I nut up on her. "Alright Kristy, you gonna have to get the fuck out the cab talking to me like that."

Nothing.

I say to the cab driver, "Pull over, man."

But he don't hear me 'cause he's some type of Hindu and talking on his cell phone in another language.

I keep staring at her and telling the cabbie to stop at the same time.

Neither one of these motherfuckers are listening to me, so I start knocking on the plexi-glass.

Cabbie says, "What?"

That's when she finally turns her head to me, cracks a devilish smile, and real syrupy says, "I'm sorry, Jude. I was just playing."

I say to the cab driver, "Nothin'," then say to her, "Motherfucker, you better be."

She's like, "God, I'm sooorry. Don't be so sensitive."

I'm shaking my head, these motherfucking white girls don't know how to act. I prolly woulda kicked her ass out the cab if I hadn't just popped this five-dollar dick pill.

We get home, she throws her shit on the couch and goes to my room.

We're making out on the bed when she hits me with, "You know, you'll only be the third guy I've slept with for free…"

I say to the porn chick, "Wow, that means a lot. Thank you."

She's kisses my neck and says, "Yeah."

I wait a beat then ask, "So, uh, how many dudes you fuck all-together then?"

She's thinking, "I don't know, like a hundred–hundred fifty?"

I say, "So that'll make me only the hundred and fifty-third guy you ever fucked. What can I say? I'm honored."

She slaps my arm. "You're such a dick. You're the third civilian!"

I can't help myself. I'm laughing, "That doesn't undo all the other dudes' come that's landed on your face."

Oh, she doesn't like that joke. She shuts down. I walk it back, I'm kissing her neck trying to talk her down.

"Nah, girl, for real. I'm honored."

She finally forgives me and five minutes later we're making out again.

It's going cool, but every time I get hard she pushes me away, pretends like she's going to sleep, waits a minute, then rubs her ass on my dick again.

This off-and-on shit goes for a half an hour, it feels like high school. I'm getting annoyed. She does it one last time. I hop out of bed.

I'm looking out the window onto my street down at the trannies turning tricks on the corner, and the bridge and tunnel kids drunk on the sidewalk. Some chick's crying about her friend who ditched her for a dude. She's sitting on the curb in a red dress, missing a shoe.

It's getting late. I'm tired. I want this one gone.

Porn chick says, "Come back to bed, Jude."

For what? So I can get blue balls?

I say, "You know what, Kristy? This isn't working. Maybe you should just leave."

We stare at each other; she's lying in bed, glowing orange from the street light shining through the window.

She coos, "Come lie down."

I say, "Nah."

She sits up in bed and with ice in her voice, says, "Come lie down or I will fucking kill you."

She's not smiling. I believe her. Not that she can, I'll beat the breaks off of her, but that she'll try.

I don't really negotiate with terrorists and I should put her out the house. But I'm thinking I'll never hear the end of it from Chris if I fist-fight some porn chick over a death threat at three in the morning.

So I do as she tells me. I get back in bed, and a half-hour later I fuck her. Every time she's about to come she stops me. And every time I'm about to come she does the same.

This goes on for an hour. She's dry and we're hot. My room smells like latex and old pussy.

After she pushes me off for like the tenth time, I say, "Are you even enjoying yourself?"

She says, "Yeah. Kind of."

This needs to end. But as long as my dick can get hard, it won't.

I'm like, I gotta sneak a nut before she can stop me. But that's easier said than done because I literally hate fucking this girl.

She usually pushes me off when I'm pounding it out. So I get deep in her and I go real slow. I'm barely moving my hips. I got my eyes closed tight, I'm concentrating. I keep switching rhythms to throw her off.

I'm edging. I'm almost there.

I feel her palm on my chest. I don't know if she's gonna rub me or push me away.

I go for it. I hit her with a jab jab jab sloooow.

And I finally get there.

I come with a whimper. Like a squirrel dying.

She like, "What was that?"

I roll off. I say, "I nutted."

She says, "Well, I didn't."

I say, "I know."

I get up, go to the bathroom, wash my dick off, and go to bed.

I wake up the next morning to her leaning over me, watching me sleep.

She says, "Last night was fun, I had a really good time."

I lie, "Yeah. Me too."

She's like, "I wanna do it again but maybe next time…"

I cut her off, "Yeah sure."

She goes on, "Only next time I wanna ride you with a gun to your head."

I say, "A gun?"

She says, "Yeah, like a real one… It doesn't have to be loaded, though."

I say, "Put on your clothes. I gotta be somewhere, I'm late."

We get out the bedroom and Chris is on the couch watching the morning news. Next to her is Kristy's purse with her MAC makeup and Marlboro Reds spilling out of it, the white leather jacket's thrown across the cushion and at her feet: a pair of white knee-high boots with with buckles and frayed leather.

I say, "Good morning."

Chris says, "You left something in the bathroom."

I go in and see a used condom, filled with semen and water, floating in the toilet. I flush it down. I'm gonna hear about this shit later.

I take the porn chick outside and walk her in circles so she can't find my place again, then put her in a cab.

I come back in. Chris is in the kitchen drinking orange juice. I play it off like we're cool. I give her a wink and the A-OK sign.

She winks back, shoots a finger gun at me, and says, "You're getting kind of old for all that, aren't you?"

She turns her back on me and finishes her juice.

I let that sink in.

I shuffle to my room, take a Valium, and sleep off the night before.

Later that day I send Chris flowers at her work with a card saying, "Sorry for banging random chicks in the house and leaving rubbers in the toilet. Won't do it again. Love ya, Jude."

She never got 'em.

heathen

IT'S BEEN MONTHS SINCE I talked to Taz, so when he calls I pick right up. The only problem is I just did half a gram of ketamine ten minutes ago.

I'm wasted.

My brain's like soup. I barely know where I am and my mouth's not working right. Had I been less fucked up I'da been smart enough to not pick up the phone.

I'm breathing into the receiver.

I think I hear him say, "Hi."

I yell back, "Hello!"

He says he's in New York, I'll be there in a few weeks. We're trying to work out our schedules to link. He's telling me his dates, but it's gibberish to me.

All I hear is nonsense and numbers.

This is going nowhere. I wanna tell him, "Lemme hit you back, I'm a little faded." But it just comes out, "I'm fugggged upp."

He says, "Me too, brother, me too. Finishing up dinner right now."

He's gracious. This further endears him to me.

Taz's a relatively straight-edge Muslim and I've been going off the deep end as of late, so we don't kick it like we used to.

I'm looking forward to seeing him in New York. He's running a high-end rug event out in Manhattan and I got it in my head that I'll help him plug it on my show.

Thick tongued, I say, "Whaa daay tazay? We blowid up."

He tells me more dates but I'm fucking retarded and not getting it.

He tries to duck out gracefully. "I think we got a bad connection, bro, I'ma get—"

I cut him off. I wanna encourage him and tell him that we're gonna really succeed at this rug event that I have no part in. I'm like, "Wegon getitman weegone gettid! Gah iiideas."

"Inshallaha, it'll go well, brother—"

I keep going, "Nahman gah ideeas!"

I'm trying to tell Taz I have some ideas to help his event reach new heights.

I have none.

This goes on for too long. I'm not tracking his words, but I can hear in his voice that he's uncomfortable talking to me and he's too polite to say it.

Finally, I'm like, "Aight bruh I'ma go. Luh you, dawg."

He says, "Love you too, man. We'll talk tomorrow."

I hang up thinking that went pretty poorly.

So I text him, "Tazzy I'm in a K-hole but I got you, dog! When I sober up I'ma brainstorm some shit!"

He hits me back two minutes later but it seems like forever.

"I appreciate you, Judey. I know you got me. I'ma call you tomorrow, brother."

I read it and I'm feeling a little better about that talk now.

I'm in the bathroom taking a piss, racking my brain on how exactly I'm gonna plug his carpet event on my hip-hop station. His hand-spun, hand-knotted, hand-dyed, intricate-ass, sixty-thousand-dollar-a-rug-ass rugs on my rap show. Tomorrow we got a guy coming on who's gonna shoot pizza slices at a chick's ass out of a T-shirt cannon.

I'm done pissing and I'm just standing there holding my dick, staring at the dirty hand towel in front of me, and it hits me how out of my league I just was.

I sit back on the couch and I'm thinking maybe I *can* work something out; who knows, interior designers might listen to rap.

Then I'm like, *What the fuck are you talking about? The people who buy those rugs listen to NPR.*

I shouldn't be game-planning shit on ketamine.

K's a motherfucker, that shit ain't like smoking a joint. It's a dissociative. It'll have you thinking you're a whole other person.

I was doing it watching this *Star Wars* documentary and halfway through, I swore to God, me and George Lucas were best friends.

I'm telling him ideas for his new movie and it dawns on me, I don't even know his ass. But then I'm like, I know him as a man on a cosmic level, we all have souls and that's beautiful. Then I get paranoid about Stormtroopers, hop up to lock the windows, and realize sometime during my conversation with George Lucas I had shit on myself. So I took a shower and went to bed.

I should probably pass out now, but it's seven and I'm antsy.

I feel like an asshole. I gotta get outta here. I gotta take a walk but I got nowhere to go.

I hit Eddie for a G walk. But he just shot some Percs up his ass and won't leave his futon.

Rachel texts me to do something. I ignore it. I'm not going around her like this.

I remember Alex wanted some mushrooms, I'll go run 'em over there.

I put myself together about as well as one on ketamine can do and leave out the house in board shorts, a T-shirt, no underwear, and pockets stuffed with mushrooms and GHB.

I walk into the sunset listening to the Doobie Brothers—"What a Fool Believes."

I'm out on the sidewalk and everything's too crisp, it feels glitchy. My eyes aren't tracking, they can't keep up with where my head is when I move. It's like I'm walking underwater in one of those old-fashioned diving suits. It's not groovy. It's off-beat and clunky.

There's a couple strolling in front of me—I slow down so they don't think I'm following 'em. I don't want them to feel my eyes on them so I stare at the trash cans.

This is my life, staggering down the block staring at trash. Then I'm like, fuck that, look at the sunset, that shit's pretty. They hit the corner. I hope they don't go right 'cause I gotta to go right too and that's gonna suck if I gotta keep following them.

They go straight. I'm grateful.

I text Alex to tell him I'm bringing him the shrooms.

He hits me back, "I'm good. I'm actually going to an AA meeting next to your house right now."

I stop walking. Turn around. Hit him back.

"I'll come say hi."

He's outside in front of the church. It's a hip scene, a bunch of mustachioed men with neck tats and chicks sporting floppy brimmed hats. The dudes look like they might work at a barber shop where you could sit on a Harley Davidson while getting your hair cut.

Alex is talking with this sober photographer dude I know. Every time I see him I'm fucked up. At least I'm consistent.

We greet each other.

Alex is like, "Yo, you good?"

I say, "Man, I'm gone off K."

They laugh politely.

I ask, "Is that weird?"

The photographer shakes his head and says, "You're fine."

I don't know what to say so I ask about AA. "So whatchall like talk in a circle or something?"

That's how they run meetings back in Michigan. I grew up around it. A bunch of lames in shitty apartments, bragging about how much they drank, coming up with reasons why they're losers now.

Alex says, "Nah, man. There's just one dude who talks and he'll pick on people to share."

The photographer playing with his phone says, "Yeah, he'll probably pick on me. He picks on me a lot."

I think he's a big deal here.

They're trying to make small talk, but even that's too much for me. I gotta get out of here, I'm just passing by.

Some dude with a beard walks up, stands between them, and stares at me. I introduce myself and forget his name as soon as he says it. I feel judged. I'm probably tripping.

Out of nowhere, I tell the photographer, "Ay, man I really like your work. I think you gonna do it. I think you're gonna get it."

He says, "Thanks, man, I hope so."

The bearded guy pulls them inside.

I walk off.

I got nowhere to go so I take the long way home and loop back around the block to see the sunset one last time. It's the one thing I like about this city.

I shuffle past the bars and people walking their dogs. I turn the corner and see power lines and palm trees silhouetted against the orange-gray sky. I pull out my phone and snap a picture of it.

Then I go back to my apartment, put on Leon Russell, and blow another line of K.

I'm in my chair, peaking, eyes closed, singing along with the record, *Hummingbird, don't fly away.*

velveteen rabbit:
the conclusion

EMILY SHOWS UP TO my thirtieth birthday party when I'm back in Detroit. It's good to see her but she don't look how I remembered. Michigan'll age you like dog years.

When the party's over, she sticks around. We're on the couch. She's catching me up on her last decade while Brad's in the other room sucking on her girlfriend's titties.

She tells me she's been off and on with Mike this whole time. She tells me they're over now.

Life's been tough on her.

She started doing Oxys, then moved up to heroin. First smoking it, then banging it.

She said she quit a while ago, after she shot up at a party and tried to drive home. She nodded off on Dort Highway and ran her car into a tree. Put her head through the window and shattered her little china-doll face.

She says she's better now.

Her nose was busted and her face is scarred. But when we talk, her eyes still twinkle and there's still magic there. She's broken down, but not all the way.

We make plans to do ecstasy and fuck. I'll bring Brad, he can fuck her girl. I tell her don't worry about the drugs, I'll cop.

The next week I borrow my little sister's Toyota and head up to Flint with Brad to handle the ecstasy orgy.

We pull into the driveway of a run-down Victorian with a dead lawn and no leaves on the trees. We go inside. It's a party house and they're partying.

They turned the dining room into a bedroom and put futons in the living room where kids are smoking blunts. It's cloudy and loud.

I'm talking to some cat named Ramon about why Pac's better than Big. Brad's nursing a Cape Cod with a girl on his lap. Emily's in front of the speaker singing along to Outkast.

When "Hey Ya!" is over I pull her aside.

"I thought we was s'posed to have ecstasy sex. What the hell is this shit?"

She's dancing, "Just go with it."

"This ain't intimate."

She pets my arm. "Just chill."

I lean into her ear. "I ain't drive an hour up here, just to debate rap music with some Mexican cat talkin' 'bout, 'B.I.G.'s better than Pac.'"

She kisses my cheek and shushes me, grabs my hand and leads me upstairs to a tiny bedroom. There's high heels on the floor and pictures of pixies on the wall.

I lay her on the bed and we make out. We start slow. We're dry-humping, my dick's hard. I pull down her jeans and put my hand between her legs. She's wet.

All these years and this is the first time we really made out. You can hear the people partying downstairs but it's still nice.

I'm kissing her gently when she takes my hand and guides it to her neck. I move it to her face and pet her cheek. She pulls it back to her throat and squeezes.

She whispers softly, "Choke me."

I say, "For real?"

She says, "Yeah."

"Like now?"

She nods.

This isn't how I saw our first time going.

I sigh, stand up to get leverage, wrap my hand around her pretty throat, and choke out my little fairy.

I lean in and squeeze. Her baby blues roll to the back of her head and she's gone. I'm digging in her with my left hand, she's dripping. I'm above her watching her writhe. She's wheezing. She comes hard. I wait a second before I let go.

I'm looking down at her, red-faced, laying on the bed, beneath her dream catcher, jeans around her ankles.

She keeps her eyes shut and takes deep breaths. I watch for a while.

It's lonely up here.

I break the silence. "More where that came from. Look, I'ma hit a bar downtown. Have these motherfuckers gone by the time I get back, so we can just chill."

I wait in the doorway for an answer.

She opens her eyes and sighs, "Okay."

I reassure her, "It'll be better that way."

We meet up with Josh at some dive bar. I wanna catch a buzz but I only have enough pills for our fuck-session later.

Josh is sober so I ask his girl if she's holding.

She says, "All I have is this Zoloft and Xanax."

"What's Zoloft?" I ask.

"It's an antidepressant," she says.

"How many you usually do?"

She takes a swig of her beer, "I don't know, one or two. It doesn't do nothing for me."

I'm thinking, *If Zoloft is an antidepressant then it must make you happy. So if one or two makes a depressed person happy, then four or five must make a regular person ecstatic.*

I take eight and wash 'em down with a club soda.

Now we wait.

I'm on the dance floor when the pills kick in. My head starts pounding and stomach gets to bubbling.

I fart and shit on myself. I try to play it off and do this ass-clenched moonwalk to the john.

The bathroom looks how dive bar bathrooms oughta look; chipped-up tile floors with piss puddles and pubes, and graffiti on the wall.

That's where I spend the bulk of my night, shitting mucus, dry-heaving, and the whole time not feeling an ounce of joy.

Brad comes and gets me at last call.

He's knocking on the stall. "You gonna be okay? You wanna just go home, brother?"

I'm wiping my ass with a wet paper towel. "I think it's outta me. Let's go see them girls."

It's past two by the time we get back to Emily's. The place is trashed but it's empty. We pair off and I take her upstairs.

We're in her room. I hand her a pill. "You got anything to wash these down with?"

She says, "Let's snort them, they'll come on quicker."

She's crushing the pills on a CD case with her license, chopping up lines.

I dim the lights.

"Where's your music?"

She points to her CD book by the closet. That's when I hear the pounding. It's coming from downstairs. Someone's banging on the storm door.

She puts down the case. "Oh shit."

"What's up?"

"Probably nothing just stay here."

She leaves and my phone rings. It's an 810 area code. I answer.

It's Ramon from earlier, the Biggie and Pac guy.

He goes into it, "So like, basically, I was talking to my cousin. And I told him I had saw you and he started tripping. So like, I just want to give you a heads up. He's probably on his way over there."

I say, "Who's your cousin?"

He says, "Mike. He's pissed."

I hear yelling downstairs, doors slamming, shit clattering.

I say to Ramon, "I thought they was broke up."

He says, "Pshh, yeah right fool. I just wanna let you know 'cause I like you…"

"Thanks."

I hang up. This is bad. I'm stuck in a party house in Flint with some other dude's chick. I look out the window, my car's blocked in by his. If he figures out that's mine, he'll prolly do some bitch shit like bust out the windows.

What to do? What to do?

He'll be up in a minute. I look around the room for something to hit this guy with. There's a hammer on the dresser next to a picture that needs to be hung. I grab the hammer and wait for him in the doorway. I hear him running up the stairs with her in tow, hollering for him leave.

He runs into the hall, then stops. We lock eyes. He growls, "It's you motherfucker. I should fucking kill you."

I take a deep breath and say as calmly as possible, "Look, Mike, I don't know what the hell is going on here, but if you come near me...I'ma hit you in the face with this hammer."

He yells, "I wish you would!"

I say, "I swear to God, Mike, come in here, I'ma bust you in the fucking eye wit the claw part."

Now Emily's in between us yelling. She's scolding him like he's a toddler. "Go, Mike! Mikey, leave! Michael, just go!"

He's letting her hold him back, glaring at me the whole time. I'm staring back at him, gripping the hammer. Ain't shit else to say. I kinda want him to try me so I can bust his shit.

Emily keeps pushing his chest, yelling for him to leave. At first he won't budge, then he finally does.

He looks at her, brokenhearted. "Emily, I can't believe you're doing this to us." Then says to me, "Have fun."

I look back at him with dead eyes. I haven't had fun all night.

He exits, defeated. She follows him downstairs.

I start collecting my shit. I hear him pull off.

She comes back to the room, sits on the bed, and goes back to chopping up the ecstasy.

I say, "What in the fuck was that, Emily?"

She shakes her head. "I know…that was crazy."

I'm like, "You told me you was single."

She keeps playing with the drugs. "It's complicated."

I say, "Motherfucker, if you still had a man, you shoulda just told me. We coulda got a room or something. You had me in this bitch partying with his cousin!" I'm pacing. "His cousin!? For fuck's sake, E, I gave that dude my phone number!"

She says, "I'm sorry, Jude! Look, you're all worked up. Put the hammer down."

I'm like, "Nah, hammer stays with me. I'ma hold the hammer."

"Fine. Suit yourself." She snorts a line of E and shudders, then puts down the CD case and walks up on me.

She holds my hand, whispering sorrys in my ear. I try to pull away but she stays on me. I'm pissed but I'm softening up. She puts her arms around me and she's swaying.

I shut my eyes. Man, it feels good. Like old times. Maybe it is complicated. Who the fuck knows.

She's rubbing my arms with her thumbs. Then she takes my right hand, puts it to her neck, and tries to get me to strangle her again.

I open my eyes, exasperated.

I say, "I'm not gonna choke you, girl. I'm mad at you."

She rubs on me like a cat. "Don't be."

I push her off me. She sits back down. Ten years ago, I really wanted to love this one. Now look at her, a fucking junkie on a futon.

I tell her, "I'm leaving, Emily."

She doesn't try to stop me. She doesn't say goodbye.

I'm in the car muttering as I drive down I-75, in the wee hours of the night, not another soul on the road.

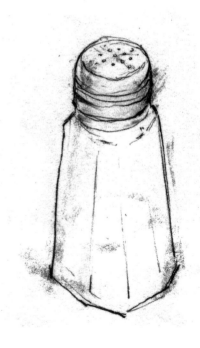

popeye

MOM'S BEEN WANTING TO eat at this restaurant for forever, so that's what we're doing. It's new, they do wood-oven cooking. She can smell the logs burning on the way to her job.

She put a little money aside for us to go. It's her, Rachel, Joelle, and me.

Joelle's our little sister. We got different dads. She's five years old, ten years younger than me.

We roll up to the spot in our best clothes: I got on Timbs and a rugby. Rachel's fishnets and Docs. Mom's straight hippie, and Joelle's dirt kid.

When we walk in, people stare. I'm used to it. I'm used to being followed around department stores and I'm used to black kids laughing at our family at the Summit Place Mall.

I'm mean muggin' 'em, thinking, *Looks like we get to eat here too*. They lead us to the back next to the kitchen.

I'm by the bus-tub. Joelle's next to me. We been bickering all night. Every time I say something she mimics me.

My mom's been looking forward to this for months and is determined to have a good time, she tells Joelle to behave herself and me not to rile her up.

I say, "I ain't do nothing, she keeps mocking me."

Joelle goes, "I ain't do nothing, he keeps mocking me."

I say, "See?"

She says, "See?"

My mom says, "Let's just have one nice supper, please?"

Rachel says, "I hope they have something for vegetarians."

We crack the menu and read 'em from right to left. It looks bleak. These prices are way out of our league.

I look up at my mom; she's worried.

The waitress comes over for our drink order.

My mom takes the lead, "We'll all have water."

Joelle whines, "But I want juice."

My mom says sweetly, "Well, tonight we're having water."

The waitress says, "There's free juice with the kiddie meal."

My mom smiles. "Oh? Okay, I guess juice is good."

The waitress leaves.

My mom leans in and says in a half whisper, "We'll just split an appetizer and then we'll get going." Her finger's tracing the menu. "Did you want the quesadilla? Or the spinach dip sounds good."

I look over at another table and this old white motherfucker is wearing Coogi and eating steak. His wife is eating linguini with shrimp and drinking wine.

The waitress comes back. "What'll you be having this evening?"

My mom says, "We'll have the spinach dip."

The waitress writes it down. "And for your entrées?"

My mom forces a smile and says it with less confidence this time, "Just spinach dip."

The waitress makes a face and I don't know if it's pity or disappointment. She says, "You won't get free juice unless you get a kiddie meal."

My mom says, "Water's good then."

I ask the waitress, "Can I get some lemons for mine?"

I'm 'bout to take these sugar packets and make some lemonade.

Then I hear Joelle mocking me again.

I say, "Goddamn it, Wellie, quit saying what I say! You're fucking nerve-racking."

The waitress backs off.

Joelle repeats me again, without the cuss words.

My mom shoots me a look.

I say, "What?!"

She says, "I'm going to the bathroom, be nice to your sister."

Rachel jumps in, "I don't know why you are encouraging her."

I say, "What am I s'posed to do, be quiet the whole meal?"

Joelle echoes, "What am I supposed to do, be quiet the whole meal?"

Rachel sighs. "Just ignore her."

I say, "Sure, okay."

A little voice says, "Sure, okay."

I jump in her face now, I say, "Hi, my name is Joelle. I'm an annoying little dumbass. Let's see what you do with that."

She says, "Hi, I'm Jude. I'm an annoying little dumb dumb."

Well played, tiny five-year-old. Well played.

I lean back in my chair. She smiles and leans back in her chair. So we're doing movements now?

I pick my nose. She picks her nose. I hit myself in the head with a spoon. She hits herself in the head with a spoon.

The guy in the Coogi gives me a look. I give it back to him like, *What?*

Rachel sighs. "Jude, you need to be the adult in the situation."

I say, "I'm not an adult, I'm fifteen."

Joelle echoes, "I'm not an adult. I'm fifteen."

I'm rubbing my temples with both hands, staring at the middle of the table, looking at the sugar caddy, when it hits me.

I reach over, pick up the salt shaker, cover the holes with my thumb, tilt my head back, and shake it in my right eye. I slam the salt shaker down on the table and smirk at Joelle with my arms crossed.

She picks up the salt shaker in her little hand, but her thumb doesn't cover the holes. She tilts her head back and shakes the shit out of it. I watch as the salt pours out slow motion dead into her eye. And then it gets nuts.

She screams bloody murder, throws down the shaker, and runs shrieking through the restaurant.

Everyone stops eating. They're all watching the dirt girl, running around tables, holding her face, wailing.

My mom comes out the bathroom greeted by her howling child.

She grabs her up and yells, "What's wrong?! What's wrong?!"

She's answered with more screams.

My mom pleads, "I can't help you if you don't tell me what's wrong!"

Joelle cries, "My eye!"

The waitstaff ushers them out of the dining room and back into the bathroom.

All the rich motherfuckers are staring at the bathroom door listening to my sister's muffled cries, and when they finally subside, their heads turn back to the table where it all started from and staring right back at 'em is a hippie-goth girl and a fat white boy with dreads.

They swallow their wine and go back to their steak.

Five minutes later, my mom comes out with Joelle. Joelle's damn near hyperventilating, holding a giant wad of wet paper towel on her eye.

My mom says, "Get your coats, we're going."

I say, "What about the spinach dip?"

She ignores me and heads to the front. We follow.

It feels like the whole restaurant is watching us leave. I'm staring down tables like I'm Tony Montana, some whisper to each other, some look at their plates.

Say goodbye to the bad guy.

When we get to our van, we pile in through the trunk 'cause all the other doors are broken.

fried

I'M ARGUING WITH EDDIE about where we're gonna eat. He doesn't wanna eat at the steakhouse we're at in Crystals. He says he doesn't like the air in here, it's too perfumed.

I tell him, "This that baller shit."

He says, "No way man, let's go."

I say, "Hold up, lemme just see what they got."

I'm out front looking at a menu, he's pacing around, complaining. The little Asian hostess is eyeballing us like we can't afford the place. I kinda wanna eat here just to show this twenty-two-year-old with a roommate that I can.

She's staring at Eddie with disgust. He doesn't notice.

This chick I fuck told Eddie he looks like he works at a record store. He does. He dresses like he peaked in the nineties with boot cut jeans and beat-up Adidas.

I laugh about it 'cause he works in finance and could buy her ass. He'd just rather spend money on drugs than clothes.

I wanna spend my money on a bomb meal. That's all Vegas is good for: food and shows. Eddie wants to gamble and this menu's too high. Ordering a seventy-five-dollar ribeye seems pretty steep just to prove a point.

I finally say, "Fuck it, let's bail."

The hostess fakes a smile, tells us to come again.

We're walking by Dior. Eddie says, "See man, I don't wanna eat here, it's a goddamned mall."

I snap back, "We in Vegas, man. They got fake pyramids and Eiffel Towers. This whole fucking place is a mall."

We push past the Persians with their shopping bags full of designer shit, out of the amber-scented air and back onto the strip to be greeted by the desert heat and fat Midwesterners nursing pink daiquiris in foot-long plastic cups.

We pass a caricature artist drawing a couple; all her pictures look the same. I ignore the Mexicans flicking whore fliers at me and focus on a train of red-faced white girls, sloppy and hooting, holding penis scepters made of balloons.

Every time I end up in Vegas, I'm like, *Why the fuck did I come here?* It's everything I hate about America crammed into one place. I look around at these motherfuckers and think, *No wonder they wanna blow up our buildings.*

Eddie yells, "Happy Birthday!" to the girls.

The chubby one at the end waves back.

I'm like, "It's her birthday?"

He says, "They're walking around with dicks on their heads, she's either getting married or it's somebody's birthday... We gotta find a bathroom quick. I gotta take a shit."

He's withdrawing off Oxys, diarrhea's a side effect.

I say, "Let's hit Harrah's."

"Sure, how about you give me some of that GHBeezy?"

I say, "Dog, I just gave you some."

"Yeah, but it's not working and the G really takes the edge off."

I tell him, "Give it a minute, man. You not patient."

He says, "I know myself. It's not working."

I sigh. "Okay, you're grown, just don't end up wrecked."

I hand it to him. He runs to the bathroom and leaves me on the sidewalk with the peasants.

A woman passes me pushing a Chihuahua in a stroller. I wanna hate her, but the G kicks in and my mood lifts and I'm thinking we're all out here doing the best we can.

We end up eating at some fancy soul-food joint. It's the kind of spot where they serve thirty-dollar fried chicken and the collard greens are sautéed. All the waitresses look like car models, overdone with fake tits.

Eddie's in love with the blonde one. "How much do you think it would cost to sleep with her?"

His couch is a futon with holes in it. He's had it since college. He's forty-five now.

I say, "More than you wanna spend."

"Like three hundred bucks?" he asks.

I'm like, "Try a g and go up from there."

He stops to think about it, his eyes close, and his head falls. He's out for ten seconds, comes to, and starts mumbling some shit from a dream.

I say, "Jesus Christ, Ed. You did too much again. Get some coffee in you."

He gets all defensive. "Dude I'm fine. I just want a watermelon mojito."

I say, "Do you see that on the menu?"

"All I see is tropical."

"Well, I guess that's all they got."

He starts to doze but he shakes it off. "Well, get me that then."

The waitress shows up and he keeps his eyes open for that.

I order everything at the same time. I tell her to start with dessert like the Romans did. The salad shows up first, the cake gets there last.

Eddie's nodding and dozing the whole time, laughing for no reason and going back to his dreams, his tropical mojito sitting in front of him, ice melted, untouched.

His head's down, he's snoring. The busboy's clearing the table pretending not to notice.

I'm shaking my head, we can't never do nothing nice…

Now the manager's staring at us so I smile and nod and act like this is normal.

It kind of is.

Eddie sleeps it off as I finish my dinner alone.

And then the manager comes over to ask, "How's everything?"

I look up from my cake and say, "Couldn't be better."

customer service

I'M WALKING THROUGH RIDGEWOOD to the L train. Big day today: Sway's doing an hour-long radio interview for *Hyena*.

I'm stressed, I got a lot riding on this book release.

I cough up a lung. This cold ain't going nowhere either. I take out a bottle of DayQuil and swig it. Get it together, Judey.

I pass some Puerto Ricans on the stoop smoking a blunt and some Russian grandmothers drinking tea. I hang a left on Himrod and my phone rings.

I look down at it, it says Ang on-screen. Pop's hitting me with my annual B-day call, where he yell-sings "Happy Birthday" in an exaggerated New York accent.

I don't really feel like talking to my dad. I mean, I'm grateful I came out of his dick thirty-six years ago and I appreciate him playing catch with me as a kid, but I got this interview on my mind.

Hyena dropped this week and I wanna get that *NYT* bestseller list. I wanna show 'em I belong.

I stay walking and the phone stays ringing till finally I'm like fuck it, let the old man sing.

I answer it.

He don't got a song for me.

He says, "Jude…"

"What's up, Pop?"

He sounds tense. "Jesus Christ, kid, what the fuck are you doing to me?"

I'm confused. "What are you talking about, man?"

"You put that shit in the book about me and ya mother?"

I say, "I told you I was doing that."

He barks back, "No you didn't."

"Yes I did."

We go back and forth about it awhile.

You tell people what you're gonna do and they ignore you, then when it happens they get mad. Same shit happened with Gabby, she won't even speak to me 'cause I mentioned her once in the book.

He's still harping on about it. I get why he's upset. He's ashamed.

I'm half-listening. He goes on, "How you gonna write that? People gonna think I'm a fuckin' rapist—"

I cut him off, "Pop, you did it. It affected me. I wrote about it. If you don't want nobody talkin' 'bout you doing rapes, don't fuckin' rape people."

He's like, "You coulda waited till I was dead ta write ya book."

I'm like, "I don't know when you're gonna die!"

"What are people gonna say?"

I walk it back. "Fuck them. That was over thirty years ago. You not the person you was then. You changed, that's not you no more."

I walk in silence with the phone to my ear.

He finally says, "Yeah…" He's not even mad anymore. He just sounds sad.

I don't know if he's ever forgiven himself for that shit. I don't know if he's ever even faced it. Must be hard to look at. They were on the rocks and there was probably no going back, but he blew up the family with that one.

I say, "Hey, Pop, I gotta hop this train. I got an interview for the book today. Lemme just blow this thing up and then we can all do good. You know if this shit goes, I got you."

He's hopeful now. "Like if it gets made into a movie, you gotta part for me?"

I say, "Yeah, Pop, of course."

He likes the sound of that. I'm his last hope for him to blow.

There's only one thing he wanted even more than having a family, and that was to be loved by everyone.

albatross

SHE'S ON THE FLOOR having panic attacks.

She's crying.

She says she can't breathe.

I'm standing over her, annoyed.

I say, "It's all in your head. Boss up, Gabby."

I leave her there in the fetal position and drink water out the bathroom faucet. All this arguing's got me thirsty.

We've been over it a thousand times: I'm only back in Detroit for a few weeks. I need to go out and see my people.

I fix my hair in the mirror.

These Arab girls are too possessive. They're too tribal. They get too jealous.

I grab the keys and bail.

I'm always leaving. Her dad left her too. But he's dead and now she's got me.

I hit the Buddha Bar with Brad and drink my Red Bulls and mingle, then come home at three and try to get some.

I kiss her awake.

It's make-up sex. It's usually make-up sex with us.

We fuck in the dark on the futon and I come inside her because I don't know what else to do. I know I love her, but we're falling apart and I don't know how to save us.

A few weeks later, she's pregnant.

We're in the living room with her mom and her sisters. They're worried. They wanna know our plan.

Gabby's on the couch next to her sister. She's scared. She's been crying. I wanna feel for her, but when I look at her, all I see is an anchor.

They talk a while about possibilities. I'm in the armchair, checked out. Then her mom asks me what *I* wanna do.

I turn my head and look dead at her.

"Look, I already got *one* kid I don't take care of. I don't really want another one..." They're staring at me in awe. I smack my lips. "...And that's that."

Her mom's eyebrows raise. She nods. "And that's that?"

I shrug, *yup.*

She never liked me before, but this cements it.

They go on making plans like I'm not there, and I lean in the chair and think about getting back to LA.

Her mom wants her to get an abortion. That's saying a lot 'cause she's Muslim. It's the first time we've agreed on anything.

Then Gabby takes me to the other room and holds my hand. She looks up at me and she says, "We can do this. It'll be hard but we can do this."

I say, "Really?"

Her eyes are red but she's smiling, "We can do it."

I'm looking back at her and I love her. I wanna believe her. I say, "We can."

She says, "Let's just have our baby."

I say, "Okay."

She's not scared anymore, she's glowing and it's giving me strength. We'll figure it out. We're smart. Maybe her sisters can babysit or something, I don't know.

We walk back in the living room holding hands.

I put my arm around her and she says, "We're gonna keep the baby."

I nod. And her mother sighs.

And a week later, we're at the abortion clinic.

It's sunny and it's sad.

I sit there with her sister and wait for them to finish.

Gabby cries all the way home. I don't. I'm somewhere else. I push it down deep inside.

Then we watch *The Royal Tenenbaums* and wait for it to get late enough to go to sleep.

They say the movie's funny but I don't laugh.

We break up after that. Then we get back together and break up again.

I'm with Julie now and I got a career. I'm having coffee with Gabby, catching up. She tells me our son would've been eight by now.

I tell her, don't think like that.

She sips her tea. She says, "You owe me your life."

I tell her, "Shit, Gabby, you're doing better than me now."

We have that conversation every year till she stops bringing it up.

The last time I see her, I finally cry about it.

I tell her I'm sorry we went through all that.

She's looking at me like, *What took you so long?* Then she says it's okay and leaves me there with my ketamine and my tears.

Then some other shit happens and we don't talk no more.

To this day, I still can't watch *The Royal Tenenbaums*. But fuck it, if you seen one Wes Anderson movie, you seen 'em all.

job

I THOUGHT ERIN WAS easygoing. She's not, she's just boring. She can't take dick either. I go down on her till she comes then she only lets me fuck for half a song. She's pushing me off before the breakdown, saying she's sore.

I'm lying next to her listening to the Isleys, thinking either she's selfish or my breath stinks.

I breathe in the pillow.

She's selfish.

She hits me the next day to hang. I tell her I'm going out of town.

"For how long?"

"Real long…like weeks."

In June, I see her at the ice cream parlor with some black dude. They look happy. Maybe she lets him fuck longer, maybe he nuts quick. I don't know.

Brandy has shitty tattoos and references trash TV when we talk. I look past that; she's got a fat ass and a sweet way about her. Maybe that's what I need, a nice simple girl. I'm pushing forty, I might as well settle down.

I try. We talk for damn near two months and she doesn't come once when we fuck. It's messing with my confidence. It's like going to a job you're bad at every single day.

I start thinking about life. Do I really wanna be going to these fucking streetwear parties with this chick? Do I really want the mother of my child to have sparrows tattooed on her titties?

I end it. She's mad but she'll get over it.

Karen's cool. She has a good job. We have lively debates. We have nice dinners. I don't wanna rush anything, but this could be the one I take trips with.

Then I go to fuck and her pussy smells like a boxing glove. I power through it 'cause I like her. I don't even trip. The vagina's an ever-changing ecosystem. I try again the next week, same deal.

That's that.

She ain't dirty, it's just her. And if the pheromones don't match, you gotta respect it, or you'll fuck around and have a retarded kid.

I stop talking to friends about my dating. They say I'm the problem.

They're usually right. I'm codependent with trust issues. I build these girls up in my head, break 'em down when I meet 'em, fuck 'em at night so I'm not alone, and send 'em home when we're done so they're not too close.

But this is different. I have good sex with the annoying chicks and the girls I actually like talking to have cave pussies. It's like a sick joke. I wanna believe in God just so I can tell him to fuck off.

I'm exhausted.

I'm home alone one night and get to thinking about Emily up in Flint. She's been on my mind since I wrote that story about her. I wonder how she's doing. I'm heading back pretty soon. It'd be nice to catch up.

I type her name into Google. She's dead.

I decide to be celibate. I'm on the couch coming out of a K-hole. I'm thinking I should travel more. If I keep waiting for a companion to do it with, I'ma waste my youth.

I look on eBay for designer bags, something elegant yet understated. Where the rich people'll see it and understand but the broke people won't know to rob me.

I get a text from this girl I went on one date with a year ago. She got drunk and started name-dropping Fred Durst. I haven't seen her since.

She wants to come over. I give her the address. We talk a bit then go to my room.

The sex is awesome. The pussy's so good, I keep checking my dick to see if the condom came off. She comes a bunch. I come so hard I start laughing.

"What!?" she says.

"Nothing, it was just a good nut."

I go get her some water and me a towel.

I come back in the room. She's sitting up in bed. I'm wiping my dick off. She starts talking about "The Flat Earth Theory."

She says, "I've been on YouTube all day and I'm starting to think the earth isn't a globe."

She says, "If the earth is round, then why do they call it a sky*line*?"

I say, "Look girl, I'm dumb as hell but I think the earth is round because of gravity."

She says, "Then explain this: why then, when I'm in a plane, I don't see a curve? "

Now I'm thinking this girl's wrong as hell, but I don't know how to prove it. I don't look out the window in a plane. I always get the aisle seat.

So I say back, "If the earth ain't round then what the fuck is it, then?"

She says, "A disk."

I'm standing here naked having a flat-earth debate with the girl who name-dropped Fred Durst.

I say, "If that's the case, all they need is a damn motor boat and a camera phone to prove that flat earth shit true and they ain't do it yet."

She's shaking her head slow. "I don't know…could be flat."

I hand her her water. I say, "Do me a favor. For your own good and mine, don't say this shit out in public ever again."

I fuck her once a week after that, until she finds herself a man and quits me.

loops

MY DRIVER'S IN A good mood, and that puts me in a good mood. With all her Deepak Chopra talk, she's got me feeling pretty optimistic about things.

I usually take my own car when I go out with a chick. But I was on my dating app, high on ketamine, and made myself an impromptu rendezvous with an art chick that looks like a little sexy elf. I'm too fucked up to drive. She's way the fuck on the west side, I'll be good by the time I get there.

Sexy elf said bring a present. I got a nice bottle of liquor in a box on my lap, she can drink that.

Me and the driver make small talk about urban gardens and shit. She's trying to sell her art and she's new to town so I'm telling her about the different flea markets she should hit. She doesn't care. So we go back to food talk. She tells me she's a vegan.

It makes sense now. She drives like a vegan: frightened and slow.

She comes to a full stop at a green light and looks both ways. The car behind us flashes his brights, lays on the horn, and goes speeding by.

Smoke blows in our car.

I say, "Dude needs to check that exhaust out."

She says, "I think he blew smoke on purpose."

I'm like, "Uhhh, yeah. His car's just fucked up. I don't think he's got a smoke button he can just push when he's angry. And to be fair, you did stop at a green light."

She gives me some silence.

I change the subject. "Doing all that driving must be crazy, huh?"

She says, "Yeah, it sure is. The main thing is, you just have to be patient and you can't take anything personal. It's one of *The Four Agreements*: never take anything personal."

She drops me on Venice. I'm looking for the elf.

I'm on some side street. It's garbage day. The street lights glow orange out here. I'm on the corner holding my box of tequila.

She sees me from her window. Her gate's in the alley. She unlocks it with a key and lets me in. She's cute in the face but way bigger than her pictures. She's wearing a dress that hides it, but I can tell. She's no sexy elf.

You see a girl on the Internet, you text back and forth with her pictures, and you build something in your brain resembling hope. Then you meet 'em in person and reality shits on your dreams. That wasn't beauty, that was just a good angle.

She asks how my ride was.

I tell her, "My driver's a vegan."

She says, "So am I."

I look her up and down. "Of course you are."

I signed up for a sexy elf and I get a fat vegan.

What a waste. If you're gonna be this big, you might as well eat hot dogs.

We go upstairs. Her house looks like a style blog. She has all the right chairs, the birds on the wall, the porcelain deer head.

It's soulless and stuffy. I open a window to breathe.

I give her her gift. She puts it aside and drinks her wine on the rocks. She offers me some.

"I don't drink," I tell her.

We talk a while on her couch. She's mumbling some story about how her neighbor wants to fuck her. I'm trying to care, I don't.

She was way more clever via text.

I ask her how dating through the app's been for her.

She says, "I just started last week. I've only been on one date, it was for a half hour but he got tired and went home."

I make a note to stay longer.

I take a sip of the G and slog through our conversation.

This one's a one-time fuck and that's it.

I wait an hour then tell her I'm leaving. I lean over to kiss her goodbye. She tastes like white wine.

The kiss lasts a minute. Let's see where this goes.

She straddles me.

She's grinding her hips. She's in my mouth. I throw my hand on her pussy, it's wet. She's moaning. I'm not into it yet, but I'm getting there. Then I feel that hairy asshole and lose it. My dick goes rock hard.

She feels me stiffen and gets up, goes to her bedroom, and doesn't come out.

I'm sitting on the couch, waiting.

"Come here," she calls.

I stare at the deer head and think about it, smell my hand, do the sniff test. Well, I already dropped fifteen for the cab.

I go to her room. I'm above her, between her legs with my dick out. She's still wearing her dress. I whisper in her ear, "We're gonna fuck, then I'ma go home."

She whispers back, "Okay."

I dig her out with my socks on. She leaves a puddle. I don't even come, I just fuck till I'm bored.

I go wash up. I'm getting dressed.

I need her to let me out. She's still laying in bed.

She says, "You should stay for a drink, we can talk."

I say, "It's late."

She says, "We can have that tequila…"

I look down at her and say, "Shit, I don't drink and I told you I was going."

She says, "Never mind, never mind." And her eyes well up like she's 'bout to cry.

I sit down on the bed, look at her. "You alright?"

She turns away, "I'm fine."

"Well, tell that to your face." I say.

Tears on the brim of her eyelids, she says, "No really, I'm okay. This just happens all the time." She shakes her head. "It's stupid."

That's not fair.

I gave her a nut and conversation. She gave me lies and tears.

We talk for a couple minutes. I try and console her. It doesn't make it any better.

I tell her I'm going. She's gotta let me out the gate. It's a long walk down.

I tell her I'm leaving out of town, I'll hit her when I get back.

I'm lying, I won't.

She says, "Whatever," and undoes the lock.

I wait for my car under the orange street light. I watch her close her curtains and shut her windows. She won't look down.

My car comes.

He says, "How was your night?"

I shake my head and say, "Weird."

We drive off.

I text her, "Thanks for the lovely evening."

She doesn't respond.

I'm staring out the window at an empty taco truck in a gas station when it hits me, I left a used condom floating in that girl's toilet.

For some reason, I feel kind of bad about that.

Then I look down and see her pussy juice dried up all over my khakis.

Well played, Fat Vegan. I shake my head and laugh.

Fuck it. I'll sleep this one off. I'm twenty minutes away from my bed, just lemme get home.

We're going north on Alvarado when we get pulled over by the cops.

He's got the spotlight on us with the red and blues flashing.

I take a deep breath. This may take a while.

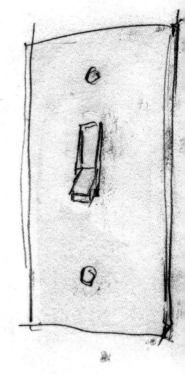

psalms

RACHEL THOUGHT JOE WAS gonna be the one. He wasn't.

He dumped her again and now she's all fucked up.

We go to Death Valley to get our heads right.

Victoria's up there, taking care of some cabins. She needs company; she just broke up with her man too.

This isn't the getaway we expected.

It's hot out here, the sand blows, and the sun hates you.

We explore ghost towns. We push our way through barricaded doors into homes long abandoned and take what we want.

We take pictures—a *Star Trek* light switch in a little boy's room, a crucifix on a baby-blue wall, a melted ceiling fan that looks like it's crying.

We're out here wounded, digging through other people's trash, searching for gems.

Physically, it's hard on me. The other day I pulled a muscle snorting ketamine. I did a rail and felt my neck lock up. I can't turn my head and lost hearing out my left ear.

I tried to have this Chinese lady rub it out but she couldn't speak English, so she just played with my dick for a while and sent me home.

I'm in pain, the heat is miserable. We go back to our cabins and hide inside till the sun ceases and the temperature drops. At sundown we take a walk through the desert.

Victoria's telling us a story about how the holy men wore linen and how it saved her dog's life.

Her dog was crippled and was gonna die. She'd been to the vet and they couldn't fix him. She was all out of money so she put an ad on Craigslist offering to trade her Winnebago to save her pup.

Nobody answered.

Then this crazy lady calls and tells her to wrap the dog in wet linen, rub him in circles, and give him magnesium.

She does and the dog heals. The lady even let her keep the Winnebago.

Turns out the lady was some scientist. She did studies on fabrics and their electrical charges or some shit. Linen's good for you. Cotton's neutral. Silk sucks.

I look down and there's her little wiener dog, tongue out, waddling through the sage, fucking with snakes. The vet calls him "the miracle doggy."

I make a note to get some linen sheets for my bed. I could use some healing myself.

The sun goes down. We lay on our backs and look at the stars. It's beautiful.

I've been in LA so long, I forgot we even had stars. Sometimes when you're around that many people, you stop being human.

We talk for a while then go to bed at ten. We're all alone with our brains and none of us sleep.

We wake up exhausted, go home that day.

We drive through the desert in silence, listening to love songs. Me and my sister, both pushing forty and still single.

She's in her thoughts, staring out the window. This breakup's got her feeling defeated.

I tell her, "Hey, you took him at his word and gave him your heart, there's no shame in that… You were brave."

She answers me with silence.

I say, "I wish I was that brave."

She says she just wants some sleep.

We get back to LA and pick up Ativan from Eddie to knock Rachel out.

That evening, I'm at my place alone, snorting K, watching an old movie—*The Apartment*. Jack Lemmon plays a lame. Shirley McClain plays his love interest. She looks like Björk. I'll probably listen to her later.

I remember when Björk used to make me think of Gabby and destroy me. Now when I hear her, it's just a song.

I hit up Mona, this Ukrainian Jew I met online.

First time we speak she asks me what kind of car I drive.

"Mazda Six," I tell her.

She says, "That's cute. That was the first car I had when I was eighteen."

Then she starts talking about EDM and Burning Man.

I say, "That sounds awful. Fuck Burning Man, we can have Burning Man at my house. I got enough drugs."

She says she's down.

But when I text her she doesn't hit back, so I blow another line and zone out. When I'm good and fucked up, she hits me.

She was tied up for Rosh Hashanah, just dropped off her old man.

I shoot her my address.

She hits back, "Be there in twenty."

Not a lot of time to sober up. I drink the dregs of some coffee and a can of Coke, then hop in the shower and wash the desert off of me. I get dressed, dim the lights, and throw on some Smokey Robinson.

She shows up in a green party dress and expensive heels. We have drinks on the balcony and talk for a while. She thinks I'm taking my time with her. I'm not. I'm waiting for this ketamine to wear off so I can feel my dick again.

I'm trying to tell her a story and keep forgetting where I'm at. Finally, I say, "I'm sorry. I'm gone on K."

She gasps, "On a Sunday?! You're crazy."

I say, "I am, but it's wearing off."

She's shaking her head, smiling, "I don't know, Jude, I worry about you."

I smile back and say, "You know what, Lola? I don't think about you at all." We have a good laugh. I say, "I got that from *Mad Men*."

We go to my room. I get her out of that dress and we fuck to Björk. I'm all stuffed up from the K, but I'm still going down on her. We make a real session of it, sweating away. I'm blowing my nose in my Fruit of the Looms and digging her out. I give her all the dick. She can't take it, but I make her anyway.

When we quit, I say, "Happy New Year."

She says, "You're pretty good at that."

I say, "I hope so, that's where my self-esteem comes from."

The next day I wake up still fucked up. I hit a rub and tug, this one works out my neck, then handles my dick. She's jerking me off, moaning like she feels good doing it. It's patronizing; I wish she'd stop. I come on my belly and bail feeling worse than when I got there.

I go to work smelling like cheap lotion and drudge through another day. None of us like each other, but we pretend to, because we're old and out of options and that's what adults do.

I finish up and head home through stop-and-go traffic. I do my chores, fire off some emails, then it's back to the couch again. I'm blowing more lines, listening to Neil Young, playing on my phone, looking on Amazon, shopping for linen sheets.

chess

RACHEL'S IN KINDERGARTEN; I'M not. I stay with my mom when she drops her off.

She gets paid to take other kids to school too. They're teenagers. Brian's black, Tim's white, they live in big houses with trees in the yard.

When we get to the school, Brian and Rachel go in. Tim stays in the car, I'm in the back.

We drive for a while and end up in the woods. We walk through the forest into a field. There are kids smoking weed and listening to rock music. We sit with them on a blanket.

The long-haired one asks me, "Why aren't you in school?"

I'm too little for school but I know how to count. I show him.

He pretends like he cares. Then he kisses his girl, they whisper and laugh.

I go sit with my mom, but she's busy too.

I wander away and play under a tree. I'm looking for gnomes in the mushrooms and moss. I find a hole under the log.

I whisper, "Come out."

They don't come, but I'm hopeful. I play till I'm tired, then I sleep in the grass.

We're back home. I'm out front on the curb. My dad calls me over.

He asks me what we did today.

I tell him what we did. I tell him about the gnomes, like the ones in Grandma's book.

He goes back in the house, there's banging and yelling.

My mom runs out.

She's angry at me.

She looks down and spits, "So you're his little spy."

I'm twirling my hair. I didn't know what to say. I would've been quiet if she'd told me.

I keep saying sorry but they don't hear me anymore.

The neighbors go in, they shut their doors. It's just us on the sidewalk.

My dad's chasing my mom around the building. He trips her, he yells. She gets up and runs. He trips her again, again, and again.

We go to a neighbors and beat on her door. She's alone, with a kid of her own. She's not happy to see us but still lets us in.

We're in the kitchen when my dad shows up outside, he just wants to talk. My mom won't come out.

We hide upstairs. He beats on the door. He bangs on the windows and yells for my mom.

It goes on forever and then it goes still.

I get up to check, maybe he left.

My mom's still scared, she whispers, "Come here."

We're crouched in the bedroom, upstairs in the dark.

Everyone's quiet. She's hugging me now.

Then I hear my name from outside, my dad calls for me.

"Jude, come to the window… Come let ya dad in." He sounds sweeter now, "Come to the door, Jude… Come let me in."

blown

WE PICK UP TINA and her homegirl from the trailer park in Rochester. Tina's up front with me, her friend's in the back between Roachie and Loc. Five minutes into the ride, Roachie goes to rub the girl's crotch and Loc's hand's already there.

We get back to my spot and the homegirl's bummed, whispering to Tina she's wants to leave. I'm trying to offer her Goldschlager to chill her out.

I'm like, "Ay, girl, it's like drinking jewelry."

But she ain't having it. She's sitting on the curb and won't even come in the house.

Now I gotta take her ass back and I got Roachie in my ear talking about running a train on Tina.

I say, "Yeah right! I gotchoo a girl. But y'all two had to try and finger-fuck her on the ride home. All you had to do was wait a minute."

Roachie waves his hand. "Whatever, you handcuffing these hoes."

I smack my lips, roll my eyes, "Yeah. Okay, dog."

Roachie's the king of cuffing.

I'm annoyed by the whole situation and make Tina give me gas money to bring her girl back. I'm thinking I got over, but Tina ends up giving me chlamydia that night.

She wins.

A few weeks later, Tina's in detention talking shit to Crystal saying that I charge her gas money to fuck.

Crystal says, "You get to fuck Jude? He'll only let me give him head and that's it."

Tina's like, "Yeah, but it cost me three dollars."

Now Crystal's mad at me 'cause I'm fucking Tina and not her.

I don't know what to tell Crystal, 'cause I'm really not into her. She's a white-trash headbanger, not my type. I'm pickier about my white girls than other races. I guess I'm just used to their features.

I only hollered at Crystal 'cause Jinx and Loc was trying to get at her. And they only liked her 'cause she had a fat ass.

Now I got her and don't know what to do with her.

I usually just listen to her complain about her man back in Ecorse, then have her give me head in the laundry room.

That was going great until Tina opened her fucking mouth. Now Crystal won't stop hounding me for dick, talking 'bout how I'm selfish.

Finally, I'm like, "Alright, let's fuck."

She says, "I can't. I'm on my period."

I say, "Well, what up on some head, then?"

We hit the laundry room.

I come by her apartment a few days later. It's bleak. No art on the walls, it's day-dark, it's messy.

A lot of times how well you do in life depends on the hand you're dealt. Where you're born, who's your parents.

Crystal got dealt a tough one. She's sixteen and has to take care of everything. Her dad split. Her little sister's retarded. Her mom's blind and deformed.

I met her mom before I met Crystal; I was taking the bus. She was on there with her German shepherd, her face looked a wreck. I made a point to talk to her. I made a point not to notice her face. We got off at the same stop. I helped her down in hopes strangers would see me being a nice guy.

I remind her about our first meeting when we're introduced. She likes me after that. I speak when I see her.

Her mom's in class now, her sister's in the bedroom. They share one. I give her sister a dollar to go play outside. She does.

We go in the bedroom. It's small and it's cramped. There's two single beds on each wall, with a pile of dirty clothes between them. It smells like dust and drool.

We make out a bit. I try to get into it but the place is depressing. It's overcast outside and it's overcast in here. I keep thinking about her sister and her mom's face and how life isn't fair.

She's like, "You okay?"

"Yeah, I'm fine."

She says, "You're not hard at all."

I say, "I'll get there."

I push those thoughts out of my head. I focus on her ass. It's round and it's soft. I squeeze it. That does the trick.

Let's do this before I lose it. I yank off her high-tops and throw them on the pile with the rest of her shit. I pull up her shirt, I fondle her breasts. I'm young, I'm clumsy. I tug down her pants and bend her over the mattress.

Dick in hand and ready to fuck. I look down and nestled between her ass cheeks is a three-inch, black, lint caterpillar. How long has that been there? It looks like a pipe cleaner. For some reason, that just breaks me. The room goes back to smelling like sour milk. I'm looking at the spit-stained pillows, a dingy stuffed Tweety Bird, her beat-up LA Gear's.

My dick dies in my hand.

I pull up my pants and leave her there bent over the bed.

I'm sitting on the couch trying to figure out how I'm gonna get out of this one. I've told chicks to wash their pussies before but they had it easier than Crystal. The girl only has one fuckin' pair of pants.

She sits next to me. "What's wrong?"

I'm quiet, I'm fishing. Then it hits me.

I tell her, "I feel fucked up disrespecting your relationship like this. You got a boyfriend. I mean blow jobs are cool but only your man should fuck you."

She thinks about it for a minute, nods, and says okay. Then she undoes my pants and goes down on me. I let her 'cause I deserve it.

Crystal's head's bobbing. I got my eyes closed, enjoying. Then the front door opens and her mother walks in. She sits across from us on the chair; Crystal doesn't stop.

So I say, "Hi."

She says hi back, "Where's Crystal?"

Crystal stops sucking long enough to say, "I'm right here, Mom."

Then she goes back down.

I'm kind of freaking out. I don't know what to do. I can't really look at her mom. Not like this. I look down at the dog, he's sitting at her feet. His eyes are locked on me.

He knows.

She asks Crystal, "How was school, honey?"

She stops, says, "Fine." Then goes back to it.

I'm thinking, *Don't blind people have super-good hearing? Can't she hear her sucking? Are they in on this?*

Mom keeps talking.

She's clueless. This is out cold. Lemme just hurry up and come.

It's hard to orgasm with this German shepherd staring at me. And Crystal keeps stopping to talk, fucking up the rhythm. She's telling her mom about math class.

Her mom asks me what math I'm in.

I say, "Pre-algebra."

"Aren't you a little old for that?" she says.

I say, "Yeah, I'm dumb."

She tells me I'm not, I just need to apply myself.

"Sure," I say.

Now Crystal's looking up at me licking the head.

I gotta get out of here. I thought I was wild but this the type of shit that'll kill a piece of your soul.

I'm talking to her mom about setting goals while I'm prying her off my dick by the forehead. She fights but I'm stronger. I finally get free. I button up my pants and excuse myself. They got shit to deal with that don't include me.

come clean

I'M DOING WELL ENOUGH to go to my twenty-year reunion but not well enough to skip it.

I didn't stay in touch with anybody from high school. They graduated and went away to college. My grades were shit, I had to stay an extra year. Then I had a kid and went to work.

Now I'm back here to show 'em I didn't turn out a loser. It's funny how insecurity works. Some cats woulda been bitter and skipped the reunion altogether. I bought a plane ticket to prove a point.

I'm at the reunion talking with people, faded on G, drinking seltzer water. I'm having good conversations with kids I forgot existed. While some of my closer homies don't have shit to say.

That's life. Twenty years'll expose a person.

The whole time I'm there, my head's on a swivel. I'm looking for Gertie. I just wanna see Gertie. See how she's doing. I close out the thing waiting for her to show, she never does.

I hope things turned out well for her. I like to think that they did.

I'm here for the rest of the week. It's good to be home. It's slow. The grass is green. The people got manners.

I'm down on Main Street in Rochester, doing the old window-cleaning route with Danny.

It was my dad's route first. When he went to LA to be an actor, I took it over. And when I followed my old man's footsteps, I gave it to Danny.

My pop never made it in Hollywood. He's back home now. He shines shoes. But he tried.

I ain't made it yet either but I'm out here, grinding.

Danny's been doing the windows longer than the both of us now. He's tired of people speaking to him like the help. But he's got a wife and kids and this is decent money that pays for shit.

Whenever I get home, I come clean with him for old time's sake.

He's got me scrubbing the windows while he pulls with the squeegee and when I get too far ahead, I come back and hit it with the other squeegee. Then he goes and collects the money while I carry the bucket to the next place.

I'm on the windows at Subway and I see a woman behind me in the reflection. She's by herself on the bench smoking a cigarette, sipping pop out a sixty-four-ounce cup. I turn around to take a look. She stands to leave. Her shirt's too small, her belly spills out over her jeans. Her red hair's a mess.

We look at each other for minute.

I say, "Gertie?"

She says, "Jude?"

I smile, "Yeah. How you been?"

She says, "Jeez, what happened to *you*?"

I'm staring at her. She's missing a front tooth, with a hole in her shirt, and she's judging me.

I'm confused. "What do you mean?"

"I thought you got out of here. Why are you washing windows for?"

"Just helping my cousin. I'm in town for the reunion. I missed you there."

She looks down and mumbles, "Yeah, I was gonna go but I couldn't get a ride."

I say, "Oh."

All these years I pictured her doing better than this. It was a self-serving vision I had; I used to dog her back in junior high, mercilessly.

I didn't fit in in Rochester. You don't notice you're broke till they put you around the rich kids.

I remember when my pop moved out there, I was in awe. I thought they all had mansions. Everybody had nice lawns and new cars.

We lived in a one-bedroom flat in an older neighborhood. My dad had the bedroom. My sister and I each slept in closets. Growing up, all Rachel wanted was a window to look out of; I just wanted some Adidas.

My dad would go shopping for me in the school's lost and found, then send me to class paranoid some kid was gonna recognize his shirt while I'm wearing it.

We got free lunch and drank out of peanut butter jars and old yogurt cups. You don't think about it till you have a friend over and ask 'em do they wanna drink out of cherry or vanilla and they look at you funny.

And you gotta pour this bucket of water down the toilet to get it to flush and let's chill in my room and it's dark and drafty and cramped. Some of 'em don't wanna hang out with you anymore. Others are like, why don't you come to my house instead?

That's cool, but you can't wear shoes in their crib. You gotta leave yours outside on the porch 'cause they're old and stinky. You have dinner with them and they got a mom and dad and napkins and everything. And the roast is delicious but you're thinking they can smell my feet from under the table.

They're nice to you but you feel like an alien.

So when I get to sixth grade and there's a redheaded, awkward girl worse off than me, I put a saddle on her ass and ride her. Then maybe no one'll notice I'm wearing the same shirt to school everyday.

I blazed her so much I really started believing I hated her.

It got so bad that her mom came to school and she was damn near retarded too, looking just as crazy as Gertie with thick glasses and coffee stains on her sweatshirt.

The teachers would take me aside and tell me to be nice. I'd tell 'em I'd chill. And when they left, I'd call her a test tube baby until she ran out the room crying. The class'd bust up laughing and maybe I'd fit in after all.

I chilled that shit out by the ninth grade and apologized for it, but it doesn't change things and you can't undo some damage.

I tell her it's 'cause I was weak and a coward. And I prolly wouldn't have been such a coward if I wasn't so weak.

She says it's okay.

I was still ashamed and tried to make up for it. I used to skip class and go kick it with her in Mr. Dodson's. I'd watch her draw and talk to her. She was a good artist, I'd encourage her.

We went our separate ways but when I thought of her, I pictured her doing well. Doing something within the arts.

And now here she is, twenty years later, on the sidewalk looking homeless.

I ask her how she's been. She says she had a baby girl, who's four now.

I say, "Congratulations. How you like being a mom?"

She says, "The state come and took her from me. Said I wasn't fit."

I say, "That's fucked up, Gertie. I'm sorry."

She says, "It's okay. She's with a good family now. They say it'll be better."

"You get to see her at all?"

She shakes her head no, "Maybe when she's older."

She pulls out a picture. The edges are worn and it's wrinkled. It's a one-year-old in a dress next to a Christmas tree, she's smiling.

I say, "Cute kid."

"Thanks." She puts her picture back in her pocket. She hits her cigarette and drinks her pop. She says, "I just got married."

I say, "That's dope, where'd you meet him?"

"We go to the same outpatient program."

I nod. "It's good to have somebody. I would've liked to have met him."

She reaches her hand out with a pack of cigarettes. "You wanna smoke?"

I wave it away, "Nah, I quit."

She pulls it back.

Danny comes out. I better get back to work.

I say, "Hold on a minute. Lemme handle these windows real quick. We can finish talking."

"Sure," she says.

I mop the glass till it's sudsy and squeegee it off.

I'm thinking, *Jesus Christ, this girl had it bad.* Even back then you coulda seen it going this route. I wasn't gonna change her future, but I didn't have to make things worse.

It ain't that hard to just be kind.

I'm like, *I should apologize.* But then I'm like, *You already did and she accepted it. Ain't shit else to say.*

But look at her, she's wrecked. I decide on one more sorry.

The window's clean. I'm wiping the sill down with a towel. I put the squeegee in my belt and the scrubber in the bucket.

I put on my sincere face and take a deep breath.

When I turn around to speak, she's already gone.

the mongol

NATASHA WON'T LET GO of the fact I threw a diamond when I shoulda thrown a heart and set us back seventy points. I'm trying to tell her it's 'cause I'm really fucked up off this science drug. I could barely see shapes; all I saw was colors. We'll get 'em next game, I can feel it wearing off already.

I say, "Let's just take this as an opportunity to get comfortable with each other, see how we play together."

Ross is in her ear, "I don't know, y'all probably coulda won this game if he ain't fuck that hand up."

She's biting her lip, nodding. I can see the wheels in her head turning.

I say, "Natasha, don't listen to that motherfucker, he's on the other team. We need to stick together. Let them fall apart."

Toni gulps down her rum. I'm sobering up and they're getting drunker. We'll get 'em yet.

Ross grins at me, gets back in her ear and says, "Coulda won though…"

I shake my head. "You motherfucker…"

That's why we can't keep a fourth man in our card game. We bring a brand of shit talking common in Pontiac, but unseen in these parts of LA.

Jeff ran Spades with us once. He brought over fancy whiskey and hazelnuts. By 10:30 p.m. we're all wasted, arguing over cards. Jeff's sitting there quietly eating nuts. That was the last time he played.

Me and Natasha are getting mopped up. I ain't seen more than two spades in my last three hands. We're going blind, getting set. Ross is laughing and drinking all the whiskey. Toni's pleased with herself too.

Natasha's fuming. She keeps talking about the renege. That was like six hands ago. I don't even bring up the fact she's been cutting my queens, wasting spades, fucking up books. I'm just trying to take this beating like a man.

In a calm moment, Natasha says, "My parents used to play cards and some nights they'd have to sleep in separate rooms afterwards."

I say, "Clearly."

I'm guessing her mom's a real ballbuster. I don't understand that: how you punk on your guy all day and then fuck him at night? Face in his crotch, knowing you're the brains of the operation.

She's still shitting on me and I don't know if I'm being gracious or a bitch. As a man, do I check her or do I just smile and take it?

I think about what Z would do. He knows grace.

One time we're at a steak dinner talking politics with a client and it gets heated. The dude buying tells Z to be quiet 'cause he don't know nothing about Afghanistan. Z's from there, he reads *The Economist*, he knows a lot.

I'm ready to flip the table over, cuss this dude out, and bail. But Z sits there, crosses his legs, folds his hands on his thigh, and leans in closer to him. He's smiling, he don't mean it, but the guy can't tell, he's rolling his eyes going on about it.

I follow Z's lead 'cause I'm his guest, I smile and nod too. I guess this is what grown-ups do: eat shit and smile doing it.

So now I'm at the table trying to be like Jesus and turn the other cheek. And Natasha's yammering on about my ineptitude. I'm thinking, *It's easy to be the bigger person when God's your dad and you can come back from the dead and shit.*

Game over, we lose by two hundred. Let's run 'em back.

We play again.

We're finally catching some cards. We're cracking their heads now.

They're drunk and imploding. Ross is scolding Toni for not bidding right. Toni's clamming up and bids worse the next time. My science drug is all the way wore off, I'm sober. The only problem is, now Natasha's drunk too.

She's really feeling herself, slapping cards down. "Okay, it looks like we're going to win this match. We had the chance to win two matches, if Jude hadn't blown it that one hand. You know which ones are the diamonds now, right?"

Ross laughs a little too loud. "Aaaaaaah!!"

I shake my head. "Don't hype her up, man." I look at Natasha. "I swear to God that's the last time you bring that shit up. I already apologized twice."

The very next hand, she fucks up then cusses me out for it. I snap. I stop being Jesus and tell her about herself. It's 10:30 p.m. and we're arguing over cards. By eleven the house is clear.

I'm drinking poppy tea, thinking about what makes a man. I don't know, but I like the tea.

It's like drinking a Vicodin.

It's the same shit that opium comes from. You gut the pods, dump out the seeds, grind up the pods, steep those in water, and that'll getcha high.

It's weird when you think about it, one part of the plant is a narcotic and the other part goes on bagels.

First time I try it, I'm in New York with Brad. We got the tea in Snapple bottles, sipping it like it's lean, cruising through Manhattan with a monster buzz. We start arguing on the comedown and drink some more.

I fly out at 8:00 a.m. on Saturday. I don't wanna waste any so I pound the bottle in the cab on the way to JFK. I'm in the line for security, nodding off, but I'm dressed like a science teacher so I get through.

The hangover's brutal, two days of aches and being irritable. I quit it for a while, but jumped back on the tea during the pill drought.

Before I know it, it's 4:00 a.m. Time for bed, but I'm too wired to sleep.

I'm listening to a history podcast on the Mongols. They're talking about some Russian city that defied 'em and lost. They took the survivors, made 'em dig a trench, stacked them on top of each other in the hole, then had dinner on top of 'em and crushed 'em to death. Turned 'em into a floor.

I like the Mongols. It's nice to hear it's not just white people who were into raping and taking people's shit.

I'm dozing off and waking up to more Mongolian atrocities. I hear Rachel come in from her man's house. My room is dark but the sun is out, a sliver of light shines across my bed through a crack in the curtains.

Maybe I'll get up. I look at the time, it's six in the morning. Fuck that. I shut my eyes and go back to the Khans. I wonder what I woulda done if those motherfuckers showed up outside of my city. Prolly gone out like a bitch, run and got slaughtered anyway.

Am I a coward? It's hard to tell in this day and age, we never get tested.

I fall asleep on that thought. I wake up to my sister in my bedroom. My eyes are closed but I can hear her moving. It's not like her to just walk in and not knock, I'm too grimy for that. Some things you can't unsee.

I'm 'bout to ask her what she wants. I open my eyes and there's a shape at the end of my bed. I can't make it out. I squint to focus and it's not my sister. It's a man. There's a man in my room.

I don't think, I freak. I jump out of bed and attack him.

"You motherfucker!" I yell. "Get the fuck outta my house!"

I snatch him up and run him into the wall. He's scared, I don't think he saw me lying there. He's not even fighting back. I don't give a fuck what he's doing, I just want him out of my house and I wanna hurt him on the way out.

My kitchen's big, I run him through it and smash his head into the cupboard. I bang it in a few more times, calling him a bitch every time his head hits the door, dishes clattering.

"Bitch! Bitch! Bitch!"

Now he's broken-English begging, sounds like he's some type of Spanish. "Ples, ples…ples!"

I run his face into a couple more doorways on the way out.

We're on the side of my house in the driveway. Making a racket in the morning sun. But none of my neighbors come out 'cause no one sticks together.

I got him hemmed up on the wall, swinging like an orangutan. He's got his head covered; he stopped begging, now he's apologizing.

"I'm soooorry, I'm sooooorry."

"Fuck you, bitch! You up in my fuckin' house!"

There's a five-foot drop on the other side of the wall. I decide I'm gonna throw him over it on his skull. I lift him, I got him halfway over when Rachel comes out the back hollering.

"Jude, what's going on!? You okay!?"

I stop what I'm doing, I look back. "This motherfucker broke in the crib. Call nine-one-one!"

She runs back in the house. Now instead of doing, I'm thinking. And I'm thinking, *If I throw this motherfucker over the wall, he might get away. So I better hold him.* The problem is he's halfway over the wall already and I gotta hold his weight.

His back's to me, I got him in my arms. I'm spooning him.

He keeps on with his sing-songy sorrys.

"I'm soorrrrry."

Holding this little asshole, I see him for the first time. A Mexican tweaker, he looks about twenty, probably been up all night. He's got a thin mustache and acne. He's holding wire-framed glasses in his right hand away from his body, so they don't break. I can smell the cigarette smoke on his hoodie. I can smell his bug spray cologne. There's a clump of dried gel in the hair on the back of his head. I can feel him breathing.

I get an adrenaline dump. I go weak.

I'm gonna have to hold this guy for a long time before the cops come. I don't even like the fucking cops.

This is some bullshit. I thought I was like the fourth generation of white motherfuckers to come gentrify this area. Looks like I'm only the second. I shoulda known that when some asshole stole my garden hose the third day I was here.

I didn't even wanna move here. But I had to leave my old spot on Melrose because some bleeding-heart liberals set up a needle exchange on my block and it got taken over by hobos and meth heads. I was tired of coming outside in the morning to busted-out windows and human shit right next to the dog shit on the sidewalk.

They don't got a word for that though, *When poor motherfuckers come to the neighborhood and ruin things.*

I sigh.

Now the tweaker's singing sorrys in hushed tones, like a lullaby.

I feel his body weight shift to the other side of the wall and fall over slowly. I got two fistfuls of hoodie and he's hanging there.

He whispers like he's cooing a baby, "Soooorry, I sorry. So soooorry."

His body goes limp and dead-fishes out of his sweatshirt, out of my grip, and slides onto the concrete on the other side of the wall. I watch him fall and land on the sidewalk. I hold his hoodie as he staggers down the walkway into the street.

I throw down his shirt and say, "That's right motherfucker, you better run."

He turns around, sees the hoodie lying on the sidewalk, comes back, grabs it, and stumbles away.

rocky III

I WAKE UP WITH my dick stuck to my boxers. Prolly just a wet dream. I haven't had one of those in a while. Then I take a leak and it feels like I'm pissing espresso. That Thai chick from the trailer park burnt me.

I ain't even mad. She had good pussy; it was worth it.

I get dressed, throw on my shearling, and head to the clinic before my shift at Cooker's starts.

The free clinic takes forever.

I'm stuck in the waiting room sitting next to this couple listening to them talk 'bout Wiccan spells. The warlock's going on about turning some rival hedge witch into a statue. I'm thinking, *If this dude's a wizard, what the fuck they doing here? How come he can't just magic the VD out of his dick?*

Annoyed, I turn my back to 'em and see this big black motherfucker sitting across in the corner.

I'm trying not to stare, but I know I know him. It takes a second to get there. Then it hits me—that's Quan. He looks giant sitting in that plastic chair.

I ain't seen him in a minute. The years have been hard on him. His haircut's busted, his clothes are out of style, and he looks meaner than ever.

He's looking at me too, trying to place me. I'm older now. My balls have dropped, I'm not a fat little kid no more.

I'm waiting for him to figure it out and have my moment of triumph.

He never gets there, so real dry, I say, "What up, Quan?"

It takes a second, then I see it register, and he nods, "What up."

I say, "Where you been at?"

He says, "Locked up."

I nod. "How long?"

He says, "Ten months this time."

I say, "Welcome back."

We're quiet.

Then I say, "Yeah, this Thai chick burnt me."

And he just looks at me—that's it.

We sit in silence staring off in the distance. Then they call his name and he leaves.

I watch him go.

I'm looking at that empty chair again, thinking about Quan. Man, I haven't thought about him in a minute.

I start daydreaming about him, about that ass-whoopin' he gave me.

Can I see him with my hands now? Nah, probably not. Maybe I'll go outside, get a big-ass rock from by the flagpole, hide on the side of the vestibule, and sneak him with it when he comes out.

I'm thinking about cracking his skull, his blood on the concrete, and my getaway route. And when he's down, maybe I'll stomp him in his face and spit on him. I probably won't be able to go to Velvet Lounge for a while, a lot of the south side dudes be there on Sundays.

I'm rocking in my chair. That's what I'll do. I'll settle the score. See how he likes it. But first, I gotta handle this chlamydia.

Then the nurse calls my name and takes me to the back. She sticks a Q-tip in my dick hole and makes me pee in a cup. She gives me this banana-flavored drink with a bitter aftertaste and tells me I can't fuck for a week.

She gives me condoms and sends me away.

I go home. I put on my tie and my apron. I go to work and bring families spinach-artichoke dip for 10-percent tips.

I save up my tips and I leave this town. Then I save some more and I leave Michigan for good.

That was a long time ago. I been in LA for years now and I'm still homesick.

I'm shining my shoes, talking to Dont on the phone. He's catching me up on what's happening in Pontiac.

He's real upset. He says, "The other day, Quan was robbing a store on Opdyke. And when he came out, the cops was there and shot him."

Dont sounds like he's about to cry, he says, "They ain't have to do him like that, man. They killed him, man…Quan's dead."

I let that sink in.

I say, "Oh well."

Then spit on my shoes and finish buffing my wingtips.

abraham

I'M IN THE HOLLYWOOD Hills, talking to my dad's AA buddy. He acts in films, he bought his house with movie money.

Gabby's sitting next to me. I got my feet up. I'm drinking the lemonade his wife brought me.

I like what he's got going on here. I think I'ma get some too. I tell him I'ma move out here myself.

He says, "Oh yeah? Whatcha gonna do when you get to LA?"

I say, "Blow up."

He's eyeballing me. "How you gonna do that?"

I smack my lips. "I don't know, just blow up."

He laughs. "Blow up, huh? Good luck with that."

I raise my glass and say, "Thanks, Mike."

I drink my lemonade, thinking he can suck my dick.

Two years in LA and I'm dead broke. Gabby and I broke up. I got a tooth rotting out in my head and when I open my mouth, you can smell it.

I was s'posed to be on TV by now.

I'm not. I'm a dishwasher and I can't make rent.

I'm taking the bus to work, sitting across from this cholo tongue-kissing his girl and mean-mugging me at the same time. I look off to the side to give 'em their privacy and there's a fat lady next to him. She's sitting there smiling, wearing reindeer antlers, it's Christmas.

I'm thinking, *Where the fuck am I?*

It's hopeless. I'm done. I'ma go back to Detroit a failure.

I woulda split if I had the money to leave. But I don't, so I stay and get that radio job a month later and move to New York.

I'm out there getting it for three years. Then I meet Julie and move back to Cali for her.

I wanna grow up. I'm wearing loafers trying to be a man, but I don't know how.

I got a career, I got a girl. I'ma start a family. I'll have a relationship with this next kid.

Me and Julie keep fighting and tearing each other down. We're breaking up and making up with new scars every time.

We're in another fight. I'm feeling slighted over some dumb shit.

Julie's exasperated, saying, "Why can't we just be kind to one another?" She touches my arm. "Be kind."

I pull away. "'Cause you ain't never wrong, Julie." I'm mean-muggin' her. "I don't know why you always wanna argue wit me, I do this shit for a living. You not gon' win."

She's crying. I'm shaking my head thinking she's dumb and don't get it. She's not dumb, she's just passive aggressive.

I'm not good at arguing, I'm just insecure. And we stay beating each other up until finally, I just quit.

Now she's gone and I'm left in LA driving back and forth to a job I don't like. Every day, passing the bars and grocery stores where we had our blowups. It's the trail of tears and this place ain't home.

I think back to my first trip to LA. It's me, Rachel, and Gabby; we're at some coffee shop in Toluca Lake. There's an open mic night going.

Some guy's next to the counter, holding an acoustic guitar. He's got a ponytail. He's wearing cargo pants with a cell phone clipped to his belt. He looks like a volunteer fireman.

Front row, at a table, is his family. The kids are hitting each other with Happy Meal toys. The wife's trying to calm the kids and watch him at the same time. You can tell she loves him, but she wants to be home.

He leans into the mic and says, "Here's a song about regret."

He closes his eyes, strums his guitar, and starts singing like he means it.

The shit's embarrassing.

I'm laughing as we walk out. I'm thinking, *This lame gave up on his dreams just to make a family.*

I'm sipping my chai tea, I got my hand on Gabby's ass.

I'm shaking my head. Nope, not me. I ain't giving up shit.

I'm gonna have it all.

on some
faraway beach

MY DAY STARTS OFF with The Velvet Underground and black coffee.

Ross gets here at seven. We do push-ups and complain about how the youth are pussies.

It's been on my mind since I seen my kid. That's what they're teaching her in college: to be soft.

They're all middle class and marginalized. Everyone's owed something, but no one's giving up shit. These rich motherfuckers'll pat you on the head and tell you you're a victim, then give that job to their buddy's son.

I told her she better put that out of her mind and focus on getting it herself.

I'm complaining to Ross but I can't even get mad at her. I didn't raise her. I'm a sperm donor. I show up a few times a year with my ideas and expect her to live by 'em.

It's not fair, I know. But this world is tough. We're still savages, we just got better at hiding it.

I just want her to be ready.

Ross leaves. I get ready. I go to work. I deal with my inept coworkers who wouldn't be working if they didn't know somebody.

It's frustrating, it's not fair. I used to lose sleep about that fair shit.

Then a few years ago, I watched this lion eat a zebra on TV. And it hits me: ain't shit in this world fair, just make sure you're not the zebra when it's dinner time.

That's life. Be patient.

Go home.

I'm in my chair blowing lines, listening to Townes Van Zandt "Waiting Around to Die." I'll take it easy today, I won't do too much ketamine today. Kill yourself a little bit at a time so you don't kill yourself all the way.

I take it slow.

I'm two hours in and the buzz is fine, but more is always better. I drink some GHB and wait for that to interact.

The G kicks in. It's good.

I'm on my phone on a dating site, texting with this girl, waiting for her to hit me back. She never does. Now I'm having imaginary arguments with her about it in my head.

Yeah, I'm a functioning drug addict, but you're a failed actress with a jewelry line. I'm still the catch in this situation. I wish she was smart enough to know that. I wish she would hit me back.

I wish this K hit harder. I don't know if it's the batch or my tolerance. Probably both.

Fuck it, this girl's not talking to me, I don't need motor skills to text anymore. I dump out the rest of the bag, crush it with a bus pass, and chop up two monster piles. I snort 'em both with no ceremony.

Clean plate club.

Once I get 'em in me, I start thinking that might've been too much.

That's how it happens: on some humdrum Tuesday night, you're sitting alone by yourself, watching medieval fantasy movies, then you go a little too hard with the drugs, and you break your brain.

I thought I was just gonna take it easy tonight.

Ain't nothing easy about me.

My old man's the same way. He can't have just one piece of cake. He eats the whole thing, mushes it in a salad bowl with a half-gallon of ice cream, and kills it in one sitting.

Then he complains when my sister calls him fat, talkin' 'bout, "Why you always picking on me? Tell me I got nice shoulders or somethin'."

I'm my father's son. I do all the K in the house and cry about being single.

K's kicking in. I feel myself go. I turn off the TV and put on a record while my hands still work. I stagger back to the couch and then I'm gone.

I can't really describe this one, it's muddy. I got tunnel vision. My eyesight's blurred. I'm confused and paranoid. No visuals, it looks dark and it feels sharp.

This batch of K is bullshit. It's like blowing an anxiety attack. I've done more drugs before and felt better, but every bag's a crap-shoot.

Just ride it out, Jude. Listen to the music; Brian Eno, he'll get you through.

I'm on the couch, eyes closed, hallucinating that I'm in some Machiavellian situation at my job. This is a real kick in the balls 'cause I did the drugs to forget that place.

I'm stuck.

Walk it off. I go to the bathroom and throw water on my face. *Get a hold of yourself.* I'm looking in the mirror, dripping. My pop liked PCP and I like ketamine. I guess neither one of us really wanted to stay in this world.

Ever since I was a kid I been trying to get out of here, climbing into an empty toy box trying to go to some magical place. Thirty-five years later, I'm doing the same shit.

Is that learned or hereditary? I wonder if Assia's got it too. I wonder if it goes dark for her.

I hope not.

I'm back in the living room. The record stops and the silence is deafening. There's no music to guide you through. It's just you and your thoughts.

I bet this is what space sounds like.

I'm past the K-hole. I'm in some other place. I'm in my body but I'm out of my head. I was stuck here for weeks after the PCP overdose. You feel isolated. You move slow but you get used to it. The brain adjusts, it's resilient.

I wonder how long I'll be here this time.

A night? A day? A week?

I can hear my neighbors talking in the hallway, they're going to dinner, carrying on with their evening. The woman's laughing at something the man said.

That's when I have my conversation. The one I've had in my head countless times.

If you get stuck like this, it's no big deal. You finish your book, you get your affairs in order, then you blow your fucking brains out.

It's settled.

I'd rather be dead than retarded.

Shit, I'll probably sell more books dead anyway. Maybe then I'll finally get some shine from NPR. You gotta be a Yaley or a Mexican lesbian to get love from those assholes.

It's nice to have a plan.

I got work to do. I gotta book to write. I got a lot of feelings in me, I gotta get 'em out.

I get up and stagger to my computer. I can't see the keys; my fingers feel like toes. I mash on the keyboard.

I'm fucked up but I'm inspired—this is my ticket out.

A half hour later, I stop and admire my work. It takes everything in me just to focus. Let's see this masterpiece.

I read it and laugh. It's just a line of misspelled gibberish with some pathetic shit at the end that says "alone."

tainted

THE MOLLY HASN'T WORKED for years. I'm all out of happiness. There's no euphoria, just a body buzz.

She's going down on me. I make her gag till her eyes water. Something about a woman's tears makes my dick hard, but I still can't come.

So she rubs my chest and fake moans while I jerk off to public humiliation porn.

I nut on my stomach and wipe up with my pajama bottoms.

She stays the night and leaves in the morning.

It's the most intimate thing I've done with a woman in years.

I'm hungover. I lay on the couch, watch TV, and order pizza. I'm there all day.

By eight o'clock, I'm antsy. I break out the G and take a pull.

Twenty minutes later, it kicks in. This buzz is played out.

I dig through my dresser for my science drugs and find the 5-MeO-DALT.

Hello, old friend, it's been a while.

I knock some powder on the back of my hand and do a bump.

My body tingles, my head gets hot, the colors pop.

I go to my computer and jerk off. I'm looking at whores on Backpage and accidently click on my Facebook tab. That's when I decide to find Julie on Facebook and jerk off to her instead.

I haven't looked her up since we split. I'm sitting here high, with my dick in my hand, coming up with reasons why this is a good idea.

She don't want you no more. Get this nut. Get your power back. It's nothing.

I type in her name, she's the first one that pops up.

I click on her.

She's aged.

She's beautiful as ever.

She looks like a woman now. She looks happy.

I think about old times. I come fast, then I come to.

I stalk her page for a couple minutes and my heart breaks all over again. She's got my number. Or maybe I'm just desperate and alone.

I'm shaking my head, *What have you done? You're conjuring ghosts.*

I'm embarrassed I did it. I feel dumb that I still hurt. I thought I was good. I guess I'm not.

I leave the room.

Her face is etched in my brain again. Her phone number's running through my head.

You're just hungover, deal with it.

I clean my house. I do the dishes. I do the laundry; I bleach my whites.

It's midnight, I still can't sleep, so I call another girl over. She shows up in fifteen minutes.

She's read my book. I'm the bad boy, she's the square. I tell her I'm gonna smash her good then send her home. I bite her ear and she moans.

I get her in my room. We fuck. Her pussy stinks but I keep going. She wants it doggy style and the scent starts wafting. Her asshole ain't much better. The whole room smells like fried whiting. It's too much to deal with. I fake a nut and put her out.

And I'm left standing in the living room. I look down, I'm in the basketball shorts Julie bought me.

I feel like hearing something sad. I put on some George Jones and hop in the shower. I grab a washcloth, lather up, and try to scrub that woman off of me.

high hopes

SHE'S WELL-EDUCATED, SHE WORKS in the arts, she's stylish but not trendy.

I like her.

There's a sweetness about her I'm attracted to. It reminds me of something I had long ago. Plus, she's got thick thighs and I bet that's underappreciated in the circles she runs in.

It's our second date, but we been talking on the phone these past two weeks. She wants to take it slow. I'm cool with that 'cause usually by now I'd have already eaten her ass, and I'm trying to turn over a new leaf.

We meet on a Monday. It was s'posed to be the Saturday before, but I guess she forgot.

I text her the day of, "What time you wanna link?"

"Six thirty," she texts back. "Oh, and I have an event at seven thirty."

"Cool."

Nothing good's open on Monday, so we pick the Thai spot next to the Rite Aid.

She hits me at four thirty. "I'm hungry now. Can we meet at five?"

I text back, "You wanna come here and walk over?"

She says, "I'll meet you there."

I get off the couch. I get dressed. I grab my GHB and my headphones.

I'm walking by the AA church, listening to Frank Sinatra, having an internal dialogue about whether I should drink some G or not.

At first I'm like, *She's tightly wound maybe you shouldn't...*

Then I'm like, *She's tightly wound so maybe you should. Plus you're gonna get faded around her ass sooner or later, so might as well be now.*

It's GHB, not heroin. It's like having a glass of wine or three.

I take a swig from the bottle and sing along with Sinatra, "Oops, there goes another rubber tree plant."

I wanna be like Frank but I'm Dean Martin through and through.

Ten minutes later, we're sitting in the restaurant.

She gets a water with no ice. I order the whole damn menu.

She says, "That's a lot of food."

We're eating family style.

I say, "Darlin', I got a buzz going and I like ordering a lot of shit 'cause I can."

The food comes.

The conversation is lively. She's a liberal, I'm a free thinker, and we keep having discussions that move towards debate. She doesn't wanna debate. So we gotta stay switching topics.

We're speaking on rent control, when she says, "I don't want to talk about that either."

I say, "Well, you brought it up. Let's change the subject then." I ask her, "You ever do hallucinogens?"

I like to recommend psychedelics to the uptight people in my life.

Surprisingly she says, "I have." Then she asks, "Do you do any drugs?"

I smirk. I say, "I'm on 'em right now."

She says, "Really?! What?"

I'm smiling. "GHB."

She's not smiling. "Are you serious?"

I slurp up some noodles and nod. "Yeah."

She says, "I'm ten years sober."

I tell her, "Congrats."

She studies me. "This is weird."

I smile. "Really? Your soberness doesn't bother me at all."

She says, "Well, I feel extremely uncomfortable right now."

I say, "You never brought up you were AA. If I knew it was that big a deal to you, I wouldn't have done it."

She's shaking her head. "It's only our second date."

I'm feeling tingly. The G's kicking in.

I say, "Do you feel weird when someone has a glass of merlot with their meal?"

She says, "No."

I roll my eyes. "Imagine that."

She goes on, "You did seem a bit off."

"Really? Why? Because I haven't been agreeing with you?"

She shakes her head. "Just more aggressive. I barely know you and you're loaded."

Loaded. There's that AA jargon.

I feel fine, just a baby buzz.

I say, "I'm not aggressive, I'm Italian. And 'cause I'm not doin' socially acceptable drugs like weed or alcohol, you got a problem with me."

She looks like she's about to cry.

She sighs. "I'm not gonna debate you on this."

She's looking at me like I'm a monster. I feel judged.

She says, "I'm not judging, but I can't even have this conversation with you while you're high."

"Why? I'm stringing words together just fine."

She sighs. "You're high doing it."

I say, "Well, it looks like we're at an impasse. You're stonewalling me."

This is bullshit.

As I gather my words to continue my rebuttal, the G lands hard. My eyes go blurry, I get woozy, I lose my train of thought.

I start rethinking things. Perhaps I should've assessed the situation first. That was a big dose on an empty stomach.

I take a deep breath. Keep it together, Judey.

My head's doing the Stevie Wonder. I stop it. I start shoveling curry in my mouth to soak this shit up.

She's talking but I'm not tracking.

I answer her back with some noncommittal "that's what's ups" and "for reals."

When she looks away, I turn my head and look off to the side. My eyes wanna close, I don't let 'em. I'm a cunt-hair away from falling out.

I focus on breathing. I snap back.

She's exasperated. "It's our second date, Jude. It's five o'clock on a Monday."

I say, "I been up since five this morning!"

Her argument was total shit five minutes ago but right now, she's spot on. I force myself to focus, I can't be wrong on this one, so I lie.

I say, "Look, I thought we were meeting at six thirty. So I drank some G after work. It woulda worn off by six, but you wanted to meet early…so here we are. I wasn't planning on none of this…"

I fight the dizziness to look her in the eye. We lock on for a moment, then she looks down at her food.

I go on, "Ay girl…I'm a wild one but I'm still a good dude…I'm like kale. I ain't easy but I'm worth it."

She won't look up.

She says, "You're not kale. Kale's easy."

We go quiet.

She's off somewhere else eating her broccoli. Her fork scrapes the plate. I hear the waitress's broken English take orders. The couple behind us talks about a reality show with a celebrity in it.

I say, "Hey, I'm sorry I made you uncomfortable. I think you're really smart and cool, but obviously I'm not for you. I like getting faded and having debates way too much to be your man."

I take a sip of my water and let that sink in. I really wanted to like this one.

She swallows her food and says, "We can still be friends."

"Sure." I say, then motion to the waitress for the check.

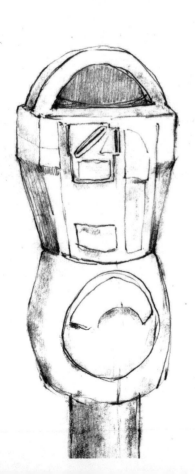

quitsville

I GO TO BED fucked up. Take a Xanbar to stay down and wake up at eight in the morning.

I'm still high. It's my first day of vacation. I don't even know what to do with myself.

I make coffee. I eat Malt-O-Meal. Now what?

I break out the ketamine and snort a half a gram. Just like the day before.

I'm stuck in a loop. We all are. Mine's just getting smaller.

This bender's been going on for damn near a year. If I ain't been working, I been high.

My brain hurts.

I'm bored.

I do another rail. My eyes go blurry but that's it. It ain't the ketamine's fault. I've done this batch: it's good. It's me. I'm broken.

No visuals. No insight. Just a loss of motor skills and bad vision.

I tell myself, *You gotta tighten it up. You need to get out of the house. You need to go live life.*

I get out the chair. I'm shuffling in circles, thinking. *What'd you used to do on your days off?*

I sigh.

I don't know, go for a walk? Call my friends? Play backgammon?

It's been a while since I've hit my friends. They're busy now, with their wives and kids and jobs to go to.

I'm too fucked up to walk; I'll play backgammon.

I hop in the shower. I drink some more coffee and try to sober up.

It doesn't work. I'm still wrecked when I get behind the wheel. I head to the V-Cut. I'll get a game. I'll catch up with the fellas.

It's hard to drive a car. My depth perception is bad on a good day, right now it's fucked. I can't tell if I'm gonna hit people or not, I'm just guessing. I swerve into the opposite lane to avoid a guy on a bike and then swerve back into my lane to avoid an oncoming truck. He blows the horn at me, I wave sorry.

I white-knuckle it the rest of the way and somehow I make it through the five miles of LA traffic just fine.

I pull up. I parallel park. I scrape the rims on the curb. I'll kill a couple hours playing backgammon. I can figure out the rest of the day later. I'm good for the next few hours.

I walk in. It's a ghost town. The place is dead.

Now what?

I get a coffee. I sit outside and sip it. I watch the cars go by. Killing time.

Phone rings. It's Andrea.

I answer.

"What's up?"

"You busy?" she asks.

I say, "Nah, I'm just sitting here, lookin' at traffic."

She starts in, "So I was driving yesterday and had a flash. You came to mind."

"Yeah?" I say.

I hear her take a deep breath. I wait.

She says, "Listen, I don't know what you've been doing with yourself, but you need to slow down. You gotta stop, whatever it is. You have a lotta good stuff going for you. I'd hate to see you throw it all away."

I say, "Funny, I was just sitting here, thinking the same shit."

She sounds relieved. Those statements usually lead to fights. "So I was right?"

I don't tell her that I'm fucked up as we speak. I just say, "Yeah. I been going pretty hard lately. I gotta chill. I guess I'm just lonely and ketamine's been keeping me company."

She says, "Sometimes you gotta sit in that and feel it."

"Sure," I say.

Life would be a lot easier if I could stand my own company.

She says, "I'm around if you need me."

I say, "Thanks."

She isn't, but it's nice to hear.

Some shit you gotta do on your own.

I been on these drugs awhile now. Stuck in this holding pattern waiting for life to get better. Kill yourself a little bit at a time, just so you don't kill yourself all the way.

Andrea's gotta get off the phone, she's got a lunch to go to. I tell her I love her.

I'm thinking, *This is worse than the last bender.* The last one was 'cause Grandma died. This one, I was just bored.

I go in my phone and erase my K dealer's number. I'm embarrassed it's come to this; I don't even have the willpower to leave her in there.

I guess this is it for awhile. It ends on the sidewalk with a whimper.

Don't beat yourself up about it. Don't lie to yourself. You go till you wanna stop, then you stop.

Quitting ain't nothing but a choice.

I don't pat myself on the back about it. I wouldn't have stopped if the drugs stayed working.

Now what am I s'posed to do with my time? Take up rock climbing?

I laugh.

I'll prolly just fuck more and buy shit on eBay.

It's cloudy out. I'm holding my coffee in one hand, my phone's in the other. I'm sitting on Melrose, watching the foreign cars pass me.

Where they going? I wonder.

Nowhere important.

I say out loud to the parking meters, "I guess I'm done."

I don't even feel good about it.

All I feel is tired.

be your dog

I'VE BEEN OFF WHORES for six years, then got faded and ended up at some call girl's apartment in East Hollywood. It smells like Pine-Sol and Newports. Her roommates are there. They got the TV loud so they won't hear her fuck and she's playing dance music in her bedroom to drown out the TV.

Her room's cramped. There's a divider next to the bed. I go to peek behind it, make sure there's no one there waiting to club me while my dick's danglin'. She freaks out, tells me to stay out of there, it's private.

I see what she's hiding. It's just some silk roses in a vase and a picture of a little boy.

We get to it. I leave my pants on.

I get home and I'm spitting out blood.

How'd it get there? Is it hers or mine? Why'd I go down on her?

Might be AIDS. I probably just need to floss more.

That apartment looked like she had AIDS. I go to bed thinking I might have HIV. That's gonna really narrow down my girlfriend options.

I wake up paranoid, hit my homie with AIDS, and tell him what happened.

He says, "It's probably nothing. But better safe than sorry. You don't wanna deal with that for the next forty years, just go get the PrEP pill."

I say, "What's that?"

He says, "It's like the morning after pill for HIV. You just have to take it for a month and you're set."

I hit the clinic and get it. I been taking it for a week. Doc says I can still fuck, 'cause I probably don't have shit and if I did, it takes a while for AIDS to kick in.

I feel better already.

I'm at dinner with my hedge fund homie and his new bride. We eat sushi, everybody's on their best behavior. Afterwards we play backgammon, drink tea, and talk politics. Then it gets late and they go home.

I'm on Backpage looking at hookers again. I haven't fucked since the whore from the week before and I'm thinking banging another prostitute might send me off the deep end. So I click on Erotic Massages. I'll just get a girl to come over, have her rub her boobs on my back, and jerk me off instead.

I'm going through the ads: it's just fake-tittied blondes and Korean on call.

I refresh the page and click on a new one. She's just my type: a little brunette, girl next door, certified massage therapist. I get hard reading the description. I steady my breath; I put on my white voice and call her.

She says it's two hun' an hour and she'll be there in twenty.

I straighten up the house, hide my valuables, take another shot of GHB, and do a bump of 5-MeO-DALT.

I hop in the shower.

Forty minutes later, she calls, she's downstairs. I put on a robe and go get her.

What's waiting for me on the steps is not the adorable brunette from the ad, but a chubby Latina with a shitty red dye job and UGG boots.

I let her in. She stinks of cheap perfume.

She says, "How you doing so far?"

She sounds like a chola. I guess we were both hiding our accents on the phone.

I tell her, "I'm chillin."

We walk down the hall, past my neighbor's and into my apartment. She's definitely not the girl next door in the pictures. She looks like she ate the girl next door in the pictures, with some corn tortillas on the side.

But fuck it, we here now.

"You want a drink?" I ask.

"Just water."

I hand her a glass. She takes a sip and puts it on the coffee table.

"Can I use your bathroom?"

She's in there a few minutes. Wonder what she's doing. I go make sure my front door's locked.

She comes out, we go to my bedroom. I give her the two hundred. I strip naked, I lie on the bed.

She doesn't have lotion; I tell her use the coconut oil on the bed stand. She starts mushing my back. It feels good because I'm high, but this chick ain't no certified masseuse.

She stops. She's antsy.

She says, "I gotta go to the bathroom, my hands are cold."

I look back over my shoulder. I say, "Sure."

She's in the john. I'm getting a weird vibe. I check out my desk, make sure she didn't swipe anything.

I see myself in the mirror on my door. My pupils are pennies. I shake my head. *What the fuck you doing man? You got Mi Vida Loca in your home, where you sleep at.*

She comes out again. I lie back down.

I say, "So when you taking off your shirt?"

She's like, "I don't do that, that's extra."

I say, "The ad said you do." I pause, "You know I'm looking for a regular."

She says, "That's another hundred."

I say, "I guess we'll just go with the back rub and hand job."

She smears oil on my back. I shut my eyes and exhale the week away.

She's rubbing me for all of two minutes and then stops.

She says, "You know what? Like basically, I'm feeling kind of uncomfortable and threatened right now…"

I open my eyes, I say, "What?"

She says, "I'm feeling kind of like in danger."

I roll over, confused.

She goes on, "So, like, I think I'm gonna just go or something."

I sit up. I'm being talk-robbed by a prostitute.

There's not a lot I can do here. I'm in a nice apartment building; I had to write a letter just to get this spot. A pregnant couple lives next to me, they're from Utah. They drive a Subaru Outback, and listen to Paul Simon. It's gonna be hard to explain me kicking some *chunti* hooker up and down the hallway at one in the morning on a Tuesday.

I can't call the cops, high as hell, with all types of drugs in my apartment, talking 'bout, "This hoe took my money and won't rub my dick."

So I switch to damage control.

I say, "Hey, let's not talk like that. Look, I feel like there's some mix-up here. Why don't you just give me a hundred back, you keep the other hun' for your effort? You go on your way and we'll call it even."

She sighs. "Like, it feels like I might get assaulted… and I really can't give you the money back, because of my agency. So I'm just gonna go."

I'm looking at her dead-eyed, thinking, *Why can't people just do their job?*

She heads to the door and I watch her leave.

I'm standing there butt naked.

I say, "Well played."

And the door slams closed.

I open my desk drawer, take out a Xanbar, and eat it.

I plop down in front of the computer and click on some porn. It's a dominatrix, making a dude lick her boot. She spits on him.

How fucking stupid am I?

I'm stroking my limp dick thinking about all the red flags I ignored.

I'm only halfway hard when I come. It oozes out of me. I leave it there a minute before I clean up.

I look at it.

It looks sad, but it's mine. I earned it.

sadie hawkins

THIS GIRL HITS ME on Snapchat and says she wants to meet up. Chicks do that a lot, but they're usually in Nebraska or Kentucky or some other place that I need a connecting flight to get to.

It's flattering but it don't mean shit.

So I send 'em a, "Thanks you're beautiful" message.

Then they'll shoot me a tit pic and go back to hanging with their husband.

But this girl's different. She lives in LA and I'm thinking that's ballsy of her to reach out to me when it actually could happen. And as I'm thinking it, she's saying in the video, "My girlfriend says I'm crazy for wanting to hang out with you…but you know…"

And I do know.

So I hit her back; her name is Claire. And we'll link up when I get home from Detroit.

In the meantime, we're talking on the phone and she says something about school and a roommate.

So I'm like, "How old are you, Claire?"

She says, "I'm nineteen."

I say, "You're younger than my fucking kid."

She says, "How old is your kid?"

I say, "Twenty. You tryna be her stepmom?"

She says, "No."

I'm thinking, *What to do.*

Part of me doesn't wanna fuck with her 'cause she's younger than my daughter, and there's a part of me that wants to fuck her 'cause she's younger than my daughter.

If I'm gonna stay single it's bound to happen sooner or later, but nineteen is damn near prom night young.

Then I figure, my kid probably needs therapy 'cause of my ass anyway so I might as well give her one more thing to complain about.

To not sound like a total piece of shit, I say the obligatory, "Hey, maybe you should wait a few years till you're like twenty-five and you know what you're getting into before you mess with me."

She says back, "That'd be cool, but I have cystic fibrosis and I might not make it to twenty-five."

I say, "Word?"

She says, "Most people with CF don't live past thirty."

And now she's explaining the disease to me, it's something to do with her lungs and mucus, but I'm only halfway listening because I went from hard dick to lung disease and I don't know how to act.

What do I say to that? Should I feel sorry for her, 'cause I don't?

I say, "That's fucked up."

'Cause it is.

She says, "Yeah."

I say, "And you wanna hang out with me?"

She says, "When you know you're gonna die, you act a little more brave. You go skydiving and try new things."

I say, "I'm not like skydiving."

She says, "I read your book."

We make plans for the Monday after I get back.

Day of the date, she cancels. There's a tear in her lung and she has to go to the hospital for a week.

Two weeks later, I check in on her and don't hear back. I'm concerned. With most chicks, when they don't reply, they're disinterested, but this one might be dead.

I wait another week and try her again.

She hits me back a month after that. She had complications, now she's fine. She's coming over next Tuesday.

Day of, I clean my house. She shows up out front of my spot just as pretty as the pictures. She's rolling around a shitty little dolly with an oxygen tank and tubes coming out of it.

I pretend not to notice.

I pick a spot close and we walk there. I don't know what the etiquette is for oxygen tanks or if the tubes are connected to her so I just let her drag it along and walk on her street side. As I hear her wheezing, I'm wishing I hadn't picked a restaurant halfway up the hill to eat at.

Waiting at a traffic light, she's telling me she's been in the hospital damn near this whole time.

I say, "That must be boring as hell, what do you do for fun?"

She says, "Being in there's not fun. But I decorate rooms for other patients to keep busy. It's just so sterile there and it gives them a bit of home..." We lock eyes and she trails off, "I know, it's stupid but I...I don't know—"

I interrupt her. I say, "It's not stupid. Motherfuckers need more than medicine to heal. I think it's dope."

She says, "Yeah, and a lot of us don't get many visitors. So they're happy to see me."

I say, "Claire, I think you're pretty fucking cool."

Then we go and eat curry at a sidewalk cafe.

At dinner we talk about her college and her nonprofit. She talks to me about her family. She's telling me how her mom's an ex-addict and her pop's a womanizer. I'm laughing.

She says, "What?"

"And now you're sitting here with me. Your dad'd be thrilled."

"I'm a cliché, right?"

I say, "We all are." I take a bite, I chew. I say, "So why you wanna fuck with me, Claire?"

She says, "I haven't had sex since I was fourteen and it was such a bad experience that I haven't really done it again. Plus, it's hard for me to meet someone because, for most people, all they see is my CF."

"And me?"

"From your writing you seem open-minded."

I laugh but I get her point because I do see her sickness.

I'm anxious. I don't even know if I'll be able to keep my dick hard. Am I gonna hurt her? Is she gonna hurt me? Am I gonna catch something? Is it gooey down there?

I say, "You gonna be able to take the dick? I'm not gonna puncture you from the inside, am I?"

She says, "I'll be fine."

I say, "Is your shit contagious?"

"It's hereditary," She says

I'm like, "I guess I coulda Googled that before dinner."

Now she's patting the top of her head with her right hand, "If I start doing this. It means call an ambulance because I can't breathe. Besides that, I should be okay."

I nod, "Bet."

"Oh, and there are scars on my chest from my surgeries."

"Alright," I say.

She goes on, "And I have an enteral attached to my stomach."

"What's that?" I ask.

She says, "It's a connector for the feeding tube. I've spent half my life in the hospital." She drinks her water then says, "The good thing about CF is from all the surgeries, I can't get pregnant."

I say, "Yeah, but you can still get AIDS."

I pay the check.

Maybe she'll let me come in her.

We walk back to my place. I got my arm around her and I'm street-side pulling the dolly.

last words

WE PARK IN THE woods and hike a mile and a half to the beach. No one's there, it's just us and the dunes; the bone-white sand, the crystal-blue water, and the green clumps of grass.

I tease my daughter as we pitch our tents. I say, "Assia, you prolly the first black person to see this part of Michigan."

She rolls her eyes, "Shut up, Dad."

I'm laughing, "For real, you the Lewis and Clark of this shit."

It takes us a while to set up: neither one of us camp. It's not my thing, so it's not hers either. I don't really do the wilderness unless psychedelics are involved.

My mom comes over to help. We tie up our food in a tree, then start a fire, go for a dip, and wait for Jack and Joelle to show.

They come an hour later and bring sausages. We cook 'em on the fire then watch the sun set over Lake Michigan.

It's alright. Roughing it's fun when you know you have a home to go back to.

Camping's making me appreciate the little things, like silence and family and not having to dig a hole to shit in.

We're all happy. We never get to hang out like this. Then my mom gets a phone call and her face breaks. It's Uncle Jerry, Grandma's in the hospital. It's bad.

We go to bed early and leave out the next morning.

We drive five hours south and go see Grandma in the hospital. She's in bed. She's weaker than usual.

It's cancer.

They ain't say it, but I know it. She's been chain-smoking Pall Malls for sixty-five years. It's coming to collect.

Grandma's not sad, she's pensive. She comments on what a beautiful young woman Assia's turned out to be. Assia stands at the end of the bed and blushes. She asks her about school: it's going fine, summer vacation is fun.

My mom takes Assia out the room and leaves me with Grandma.

We catch up and talk about family things. We end up spending most of our time trying to figure out why Aunt Lisa isn't talking to anybody. She hasn't spoken to half the family for years. It affects us.

Then Grandma gets tired and I gotta leave. I kiss her cheek and tell her I love her. I walk down the hall with my arm around my kid, thinking that might've been the last conversation we got to have. I had so much to tell her and I wasted it talking about Auntie Lisa.

I drive to the airport that night and that talk is nagging at me. What a waste. I pop a Vicodin and put it out my mind. That's how things go, I guess. Maybe I'll call her later.

The plane's delayed two hours, so I eat fried chicken and do drugs till I puke.

Time goes by and still no flight. Be patient. You'll get back to LA and away from here soon enough.

Eleven at night, we're finally lining up to board and they announce the flight's been canceled.

I rent a car. I go home.

I don't believe in God, but I pray when a chick's period's late.

In fifteen years of flying I've never had a flight canceled. Maybe this is divine intervention keeping me off that plane, maybe it's luck. I don't know what it is but I'm not gonna waste it.

I go see Grandma first thing in the morning. Before she's diagnosed with cancer. Before they say it's in her lungs and in her bones, I go see her. Before the chemo takes her hair and her words, I go see her. Before it breaks down her insides and she dies. I go see my grandma.

I tell her how much she means to me. I tell how hard it was for me growing up. How I never felt safe. How her simple gestures did so much for me. When my shoes were filled with holes and rotten, she got me new ones. When I needed a place to stay, she gave me one.

It meant a lot.

I thank her.

I tell her I'm older now, I understand things. When I'd beg her to step in between my mom and Terry, that we were dying over there and she'd be at the kitchen table, cigarette burning in the ashtray, drinking her coffee, and tell me no. I used to get so mad at her, but I get it. It must've been hard to watch us suffer, but they were grown-ups. People do what they're gonna do.

I'm okay now.

I'm holding her hand, I'm crying.

She tells me she watched me struggle raising my daughter and she knew I needed help, but she wouldn't give it to me. She didn't want me raising my own kid. She thought Assia's grandparents would be better for her than I was.

I remember that. I'm a teenager, my baby mama's people don't like me, and my own family's not there. My grandma won't even watch her when I need to run up to the store for diapers. I'm alone. I don't know what to do. I don't even want my kid. She comes over and cries, I lose my temper. I'm bitter she's born, no one asked me. Then I see this little toddler and she looks like me, it ain't her fault she's here. You feel bad for resenting your kid. It kills you 'cause you know you shouldn't but you do. And it's so easy to let her go and it's hard to see her once she's gone.

Truth hurts, I tell her I understand. I wouldn't have been a good dad.

We're quiet. I'm thinking about that. About life. What could've been and what is.

She says, "Jude, there's something that's bothered me for years and I've always wanted to apologize for it."

I tell her, "We're good, don't worry about it."

She goes on, "When you turned three, at your birthday party. Your parents were breaking up. It was hard on everyone. It was tense. Your father was throwing you in the air and catching you. I told him, Angie be careful not to drop you. He was going through a tough time. I think he felt like he was being attacked so he threw you in the air and dropped you on purpose. You landed on your butt and started crying. I wanted to stick up for you, but I didn't. I thought if I said anything more I would just make things worse."

I'm shaking my head, grinning.

I say, "Grandma. I don't even remember that."

But she does and it hurts her. Sometimes people gotta apologize for themselves; it's not for you.

We're silent in that hospital room with the machines beeping and the nurses' voices in the hallway and I squeeze her hand.

She says, "You know, Jude, you don't have to be so hard. You don't have to be so angry."

I sit with that. I smile. I say, "Aw, Grandma, when anger gets you this far in life, it's scary to let it go. You start thinking that's all you got. You don't know what else is gonna drive you."

She says to me, "Just know you're more than anger. There's joy in the world, if you let it come to you."

I say, "I know that. I'm trying. It takes a long time to melt an iceberg. Nothing happens overnight, but I'll get there."

st. jude

MY DAD HAS THE car. My mom's walking me home from kindergarten. I just started. They enrolled me early to get me away from all the fighting. It was Grandma's idea.

It's sunny out. The grass is green. There's a breeze in the air.

She's asking me about my day. I tell her I made a friend. I'm shy.

We're a block away from my house, I look down and see a penny on the ground. I stop talking. I reach down and get it.

"Find a penny pick it up. All the day you'll have good luck."

I'm happy. That's a lot to a four-year-old. I got a lucky penny.

I'm standing there holding it, looking at it. It's tarnished and brown but it's mine. I squeeze it in my hand. I take a few steps. I think a moment.

I say to the world as much as to her, "You know, Mom, I'm gonna leave it here. So someone else can find the penny. And they can have good luck too."

I make a ceremony of it as I put it back on the concrete and my mom tells me what a nice little boy I am.

I walk down the sidewalk empty-handed and proud. She leads me back to my house needing all the luck I could get.

I wish she woulda told me to keep it.

thank you

First and foremost, I wanna thank all the Sirius and Shade 45 listeners who bought the last book. Although I like my writing, I realize most of y'all don't even buy books, you were buying me, you're the main reason why *Hyena* was such a success and why I was able to do this follow-up.

Secondly, I wanna thank my mom and dad. You read to me and Rach and took us to the library as often as you could. You stressed the importance of books. And even though I was in an English class with the kids with the helmets on, I still read in my spare time, from Judy Blume to Eldridge Cleaver to Larry McMurtry. I'm not formally educated and reading taught me how to tell a story.

Now for the business end: Dennis Ardi is my lawyer. Foundry is the agency. Peter McGuigan is my agent; Claire Harris is his right hand. Richie Kern is handling the Hollywood shit for *Hummingbird*. Ally Musika pushed to get *Hyena* optioned by HBO, which made me look cool. Andrea Grano edited the last book and still gives me notes. Matt Jelmini is handling my FB.

Paul Rosenberg saved me from busting suds on Santa Monica.

Thanks to Rare Bird for putting this out. You're creative, driven, and flexible. You treated *Hummingbird* like the piece of art that I view it as and not a fucking product. Shit, what other publisher's gonna let you drop a memoir with no words on the cover? Tyson Cornell, Julia Callahan, Hailie Johnson, Alice Elmer, Gregory Henry, Jake Levens, and the rest of the fam: thank you.

While we're talking covers, Sage Vaughn did mine and I fucking love it. Thank you, bro.

Ruby Roth did the illustrations. I've admired you forever and it was great to work with you.

Jack, Joelle, Danny, Sarah, Rachel, thank you for being so supportive. I'm nothing without my family. My daughter, Assia, I love you very much, I'm very proud of you, and one day I hope to have a vocabulary as good as yours and for you to have a book out next to mine.

Sonya, no one has your grind, watching you has made me try harder and you were a big inspiration for me to write.

Stephen let me bounce my daily writing off him. Patricia's support meant the world. Alex tried to sober me up...didn't work. Diana fueled some of these stories. Taryn was in these streets. Nathan got me to start that blog in the first place. Brian, Ross, and Alan ain't do shit on this one, but fuck it, thanks for letting me talk your ears off about this shit. Mikey's my guy. Chiko used to drop me off at the hooker's spot. Sarah Saiger did absolutely nothing for this book but she's been bugging the shit outta me for a thank you.

I hope my last two books have carried some of y'all through tough times, got some of y'all reading again, and inspired others to write.

Thank you all.

hummingbird,

don't fly away.